Certification Study Companion Series

The Apress Certification Study Companion Series offers guidance and hands-on practice to support technical and business professionals who are studying for an exam in the pursuit of an industry certification. Professionals worldwide seek to achieve certifications in order to advance in a career role, reinforce knowledge in a specific discipline, or to apply for or change jobs. This series focuses on the most widely taken certification exams in a given field. It is designed to be user friendly, tracking to topics as they appear in a given exam. Authors for this series are experts and instructors who not only possess a deep understanding of the content, but also have experience teaching the key concepts that support readers in the practical application of the skills learned in their day-to-day roles.

More information about this series at https://link.springer.com/bookseries/17100

Designing and Implementing Cloud-native Applications Using Microsoft Azure Cosmos DB

Study Companion for the DP-420 Exam

Steve Flowers

Apress®

Designing and Implementing Cloud-native Applications Using Microsoft Azure Cosmos DB: Study Companion for the DP-420 Exam

Steve Flowers
Perrysburg, OH, USA

ISBN-13 (pbk): 978-1-4842-9546-5 ISBN-13 (electronic): 978-1-4842-9547-2
https://doi.org/10.1007/978-1-4842-9547-2

Managing Director, Apress Media LLC: Welmoed Spahr
Acquisitions Editor: Jonathan Gennick
Development Editor: Laura Berendson
Editorial Project Manager: Shaul Elson

Cover by eStudioCalamar

Distributed to the book trade worldwide by Springer Science+Business Media LLC, 1 New York Plaza, Suite 4600, New York, NY 10004. Phone 1-800-SPRINGER, fax (201) 348-4505, e-mail orders-ny@springer-sbm.com, or visit www.springeronline.com. Apress Media, LLC is a California LLC and the sole member (owner) is Springer Science + Business Media Finance Inc (SSBM Finance Inc). SSBM Finance Inc is a **Delaware** corporation.

For information on translations, please e-mail booktranslations@springernature.com; for reprint, paperback, or audio rights, please e-mail bookpermissions@springernature.com.

Apress titles may be purchased in bulk for academic, corporate, or promotional use. eBook versions and licenses are also available for most titles. For more information, reference our Print and eBook Bulk Sales web page at http://www.apress.com/bulk-sales.

Any source code or other supplementary material referenced by the author in this book is available to readers on GitHub (https://github.com/Apress). For more detailed information, please visit https://www.apress.com/gp/services/source-code.

Paper in this product is recyclable

Dedicated to my wife Jacqui whose love and support is limitless.

Table of Contents

About the Author

Steve Flowers is a Senior Cloud Solution Architect at Microsoft focused on Data and AI. He has 12 years of experience in technology, and for the past three years, he has helped customers achieve success with Azure Cosmos DB. In 2022, Steve achieved the Azure Cosmos DB Technical Insider badge acknowledging his training with the product group and Microsoft Global Black Belts in Azure Cosmos DB, and for helping enterprise customers architect and deploy Azure Cosmos DB. Steve's technical experience ranges from networking and system administration to cloud-native development on Azure and IoT solutions. He is passionate about data architecture and enjoys the challenge of a customer-driven role within Microsoft.

About the Technical Reviewer

 **Hasan Savran** is a highly experienced Senior Business Intelligence Manager at Progressive Insurance Company and a distinguished Microsoft Data Platform MVP based in the United States. He is also the head of SavranWeb Cosmos DB Consulting, where he showcases his exceptional industry knowledge and skills. Sharing knowledge and expertise with the community is his passion. He achieves this by speaking at tech conferences globally and writing on his blog: `https://bit.ly/44wr52u`. Hasan has also developed a VSCode extension called Azure Cosmos DB SQL Studio (`https://bit.ly/3yKWkYP`), which streamlines the complexities of working with Azure Cosmos DB. This tool offers a seamless and efficient experience for interacting with the platform, making it a valuable asset for any user.

Acknowledgments

Thank you Hasan Savran for your time and deep expertise reviewing this text.

Thank you Shaul Elson for your work organizing this effort and Jon Gennick for the opportunity.

Thank you to Sergiy Smyrnov, Howard Ginsburg, Jeremiah Gutherie, Marc Grove, Prasad Nair, and my other Microsoft colleagues who have helped me on my Azure Cosmos DB journey.

Thank you to the Azure Cosmos DB Product Group for building the best cloud distributed NoSQL platform in the industry. And thank you for all you do to train and share your expertise with the community.

Thank you to my many mentors: Charlie, Troy, Erich, Freddy, Kevin, Frannie, Scott, Ken, Edward, Sweta, Amy, Cathy, and Brian.

Finally, thank you to all my friends on the Microsoft Azure Discord server!
`https://aka.ms/azurediscord`

Preface

The goal of this book is to introduce readers to the Azure Cosmos DB service and the topics covered on the DP-420 certification exam. Whether you are a developer experienced with using Azure Cosmos DB or you are just starting your journey, I hope this book can provide valuable information for you.

Gaining technical certificates is a way to show your employer or potential employers you are proficient in a specific technology. Many exams have come and gone over the years. The value of those that fade also diminish with technology. But NoSQL will likely remain a relevant skill for years to come, and though this book is focused specifically on Azure Cosmos DB, many of the topics discussed in this book can be applied to other NoSQL products and platforms.

Some readers may also be seeking to obtain this certification as a mechanism of self-study. Having a predetermined outline for learning and a goal to accomplish such as the passing of an exam can be an excellent starter. This book will certainly help you thoroughly understand NoSQL concepts and how to work with the Azure Cosmos DB platform, whether you choose to take the exam or not.

If you do take the exam, I offer an important piece of advice that should be applied to any study material on a subject: don't stop here. Don't let this book carry you through the exam. Study the documentation. Dig into topics you don't understand using the vast resources at your fingertips: ChatGPT, StackOverflow, Discord, Slack, LinkedIn, YouTube, etc. Work through the quick starts and tutorials in the Microsoft documentation, many of which are linked in the companion repository associated with this text.[1] And if you aren't using Azure Cosmos DB in your current role, stay connected to the aforementioned communities and keep your skills sharp. NoSQL proficiency is likely to be relevant in your career aspirations. Good luck, and thanks for reading.

---

[1] https://github.com/Apress/designing-and-implementing-cloud-native-applications

CHAPTER 1

Scheduling and Taking the DP-420 Exam

In this chapter, I will outline how to schedule, prepare, and take the DP-420 exam. If you have never taken a technical certification exam before, the information provided in the following sections will help you gain confidence before you sit for the exam.

Benefits of Obtaining the DP-420 Certification

Obtaining a professional certificate is a great way to show proficiency in an area of technology. Most professionals will obtain a certificate to provide proof of their experience working with a set of technologies. Some will obtain a certificate as required by their employer, and some will use the certificate as a learning path to gain skills they have not been exposed to in their day-to-day work.

Why Should You Take the DP-420 Exam?

Azure Cosmos DB is a modern, scalable, *NoSQL* database service that is fully managed on the Microsoft Azure platform. Many developers are reconsidering their use of relational database management systems (RDBMS) in favor of the flexibility and speed of NoSQL. Developers choose Azure Cosmos DB due to the simplicity of management, ease of development, and awesome global scale.

There are topics in the DP-420 that relate to any NoSQL service such as data modeling, partitioning, and consistency. A proven mastery of these concepts will translate well to any NoSQL platform. In addition to the requirements of a general NoSQL solution, Azure Cosmos DB comes with rich functionality developers require in a modern ecosystem when working on small, local projects or critical, globally distributed

1

© Steve Flowers 2023
S. Flowers, *Designing and Implementing Cloud-native Applications Using Microsoft Azure Cosmos DB*, Certification Study Companion Series, https://doi.org/10.1007/978-1-4842-9547-2_1

applications. Passing the DP-420 exam can either help you on your journey in learning NoSQL and Azure Cosmos DB or serve as a credential validating your knowledge and experience.

Who Should Take the DP-420 Exam?

I've found that taking a certification exam provides a structured way to learn about a technology and the certificate validates my learning. As technology professionals we are often asked to learn new things and navigating the breadth of deep technical topics can be difficult when first starting off. Following the learning path of a certification is a great way to adhere to a structured approach, focusing on the core of a technology and providing a firm foundation to gain deeper insights and experience. Whether you are a seasoned app dev or looking to find a role that focuses on modern cloud-native application development, obtaining the DP-420 will demonstrate your ability to successfully leverage Azure Cosmos DB.

Even though there are many resources available to help you study, including this book, I highly recommend that candidates understand basic concepts of app development and databases. This book will make references to phrases like "primary key," "ACID transactions," "stored procedures," "SDK," and so on. If you do not understand these terms, studying and passing this exam will be difficult. The official documentation outlines the following recommendation for candidates:

> *A candidate for this exam must have solid knowledge and experience developing apps for Azure and working with Azure Cosmos DB database technologies. They should be proficient at developing applications that use the Azure Cosmos DB .NET SDK for SQL API. They should be able to write efficient Azure Cosmos DB SQL queries and be able to create appropriate index policies. They should have experience creating server-side objects with JavaScript. Additionally, they should be familiar with provisioning and managing resources in Azure. They should be able to interpret JSON, read C# or Java code, and use PowerShell.*

> —https://docs.microsoft.com/en-us/certifications/exams/dp-420

Preparing for the Exam

Preparation is key to passing a certification exam as well as learning and retaining new skills. There are many resources you can use to study for this exam. I assume since you are reading this book, you prefer a strategic, focused approach to studying. Me too. The goal of this book is to give you all the key information you need to pass the DP-420 exam. However, additional resources will help cement the information into memory, so you feel confident at test time.

A lot of the information outlined in this book is based on the Microsoft documentation (docs.microsoft.com), albeit summarized and focused on exam topics. I suggest if you are struggling with a particular topic you use the official documentation to further your studies. Be careful not to stray into the deep end, because the documentation can include depth that can be overwhelming and will not be required for the exam. Going too deep in your studies could cause confusion during test time.

Another great resource I turn to on technical topics is YouTube. There are many content creators who discuss Azure Cosmos DB topics including the DP-420 exam, new features, and design patterns. But rather than finding a random channel where it is impossible to know whether the information you are receiving is good and accurate, I suggest you check out the official Azure Cosmos DB YouTube channel:

`www.youtube.com/c/AzureCosmosDB`

Here you will find a wealth of information from Microsoft employees working in the Azure Cosmos DB product group, Azure Cosmos DB Global Black Belts (highly technical field resources), and Microsoft MVPs. The Microsoft Developer channel is also a great place for Azure Cosmos DB information:

`www.youtube.com/c/MicrosoftDeveloper`

They have created a playlist that includes videos for all the topics covered in the exam:

`https://tinyurl.com/YoutubePlaylistDp420`

Finally, beyond reading and watching videos, it is imperative to get hands on with the Azure Cosmos DB service. The DP-420 expects you to understand how to create and manage the service in the Azure Portal as well as using Azure CLI and PowerShell. Spend time exploring the portal, understanding the important configurations and how to also perform those configurations using PowerShell or Azure CLI. Make sure to write queries! There will be many questions on the exam that will be made easier by writing queries and understanding the most common statements and how they function.

Also, spend time developing against the service. C# is the language I recommend but some of the important things to know are how to create a client, working with client options, interacting with the change feed, and writing and interacting with stored procedures. The methods and properties across different languages should be similar, but understand that C# is the language of Microsoft. To develop locally, download and install the Azure Cosmos DB Emulator. This is a free installable which mimics the APIs you will use in the real Azure service.

Scheduling the Exam

The first thing to tackle is creating a certification profile if you have never taken an exam. Log in to Microsoft Learn (`https://docs.microsoft.com/en-us/learn/`) and check your profile under "Certifications," and if no profile exists, you'll need to create one. The easiest way to create one is to search Microsoft Learn for the DP-420 exam and click "Schedule Exam." You'll be redirected to a page asking you to establish a Microsoft Certification Profile. Provide your information and select "Save & Continue." For further information on this process, see the resources provided at the following URLs:

docs.microsoft.com/certifications/register-schedule-exam

docs.microsoft.com/certifications/prepare-exam

Testing is scheduled through Pearson VUE and the scheduling process will resume on their site once your profile is configured. Select the language you require and choose an in-person test or a remotely proctored test.

What to Expect When Taking the Exam at a Testing Center

The in-person testing experience has been the standard for many years. The times offered will be based on the availability of your local testing centers. On the day of the exam, show up early to give yourself time to check in. Typically, you will be asked to place all your belongings into a private locker. This prevents anyone from bringing in items that could be used to gain an unfair advantage or cheat during the exam. Your photo is also taken and included with the results of your exam. Your results are typically provided at the end of the exam and a printout presented to you by the front desk.

When it is time to take your exam, you will be escorted to the test taking room and sat at a desk with a PC managed by the testing center. You are not allowed to take anything in with you, and not allowed to write on anything other than the materials offered to you by the testing center which typically include a small thin whiteboard and dry-erase markers. The whiteboard cannot be erased and if you require more writing room you must request it from a testing center assistant.

At every testing center I have taken a test in, the room includes others who are taking exams on a number of topics. Keep in mind that your movement and sounds can be distracting to them, and theirs may be distracting to you. If you are easily distracted, I recommend the second approach, a remotely proctored exam.

What to Expect When Taking the Exam Virtually

When choosing to schedule a remotely proctored exam, the times offered will be based on the availability of proctor staff. A proctor is someone who will make sure you are set up to take the exam but also monitor your testing environment to ensure the integrity of the results. This includes requiring access to your PC, microphone, speakers, and validating the room where you will be taking the test is free of material which could be leveraged to cheat. Through Pearson VUE this requires a client to be installed on your device. Install the client well before your exam date and follow the testing and validation of your PC when the client asks. This will ensure their proctor agents can connect and administer the test reliably.

Before you even sit for the exam you will receive materials on ensuring your remote testing site is suitable. Pearson VUE requires an empty room with no pictures, TVs, monitors, or bookshelves. Your desk or tabletop must be empty and there must be no miscellaneous items around the room. Give yourself time to check in with the remote proctor who will inspect your space and advise you if anything present is not compliant. For many homes, finding such a room can be difficult. My friend and colleague Howard Ginsburg recommends using a washroom, that is, a bathroom, commode, water closet, and so on. It sounds silly at first, but if you think about it, those rooms are quite sterile! There typically isn't anything on the walls that cannot be removed easily, and most toilets are right next to a vanity or countertop where you can set your test taking device. This obviously requires that you have a test taking device such as a laptop. If you do not own a PC or cannot procure one, then taking the test in a testing center may be best.

Test Results

Regardless of whether you take the exam in a testing center or the privacy home virtually, you will be presented with the results of the exam immediately after completion. To pass the exam, you must score at least **700**. This is a scaled score and *does not mean* you've answered 70% of the questions correctly out of 1,000. Questions are not weighted evenly, and the score is designed to assess your competency and takes into consideration the difficulty of the question as well. See the following link for more information:

```
https://docs.microsoft.com/en-us/certifications/exam-scoring-
reports#scores-needed-to-pass-exams
```

You've Failed the Exam, Now What?

You can retake the exam 24 hours after your first attempt. After that, the time you must wait varies. Refer to the prior link for more information. After completing the exam, you will see a printout that summarizes your strengths and weaknesses in the various exam objectives. Consider this printout your new study guide and hammer these objectives. I recommend taking the exam again quickly if you have barely missed the mark. However, if you have failed to pass by any significant measure, it may be a sign you are not ready to take the exam. Continue to study, continue to write queries, continue to code against Azure Cosmos DB, and come back to the exam when you feel more confident.

Refreshing Your DP-420 Certification

Refreshing your certification is important to maintain your skills and your credential. The good news is this process has changed drastically over the last 18 months. It used to be that to renew your certification, you had to retake the exam. This meant checking to see if the exam has updated, studying up on new material or old material that you may not feel confident on anymore, and retaking.

The new refresh experience happens through Microsoft Learn. This is great because you don't have to schedule the exam, it is not proctored, and you can take as long as you want. You can also attempt the renewal exam as many times as you would like. See the link I provided at the beginning of this section for more information on renewals.

If you have been working with Azure Cosmos DB since taking the exam, you likely will need very little studying. If you have not, I recommend refreshing yourself on the exam objectives before taking the renewal.

Summary

If this is your first time taking a Microsoft certification exam, don't worry! In this book we will cover the most important aspects of Azure Cosmos DB. If you have not worked with the service before, this will be an exciting journey. Make sure to continue studying topics you don't understand and reference the Microsoft Docs for more information. And lastly, get hands on with the topics. Write queries, develop code, create stored procedures, and deploy your account with PowerShell. Practice will ensure these ideas are cemented in your memory.

## CHAPTER 2

Design and Implement a Nonrelational Data Model

Data modeling is an extremely important aspect of NoSQL design. Throw 3NF (third normal form) out the window and adopt the perspective of the developer, instead of the DBA. What does the developer of a critical, globally distributed application care about? Low-latency transactions and multi-write replication. This isn't to say relational databases which have long ago adopted 3NF can be tossed out with the water, but applications seeking low-latency global availability cannot be tied to these restrictions. There is of course the rise of a hybrid approach in NewSQL, but that is a topic outside of the scope of this book.

A good NoSQL data model will allow for efficient use of underlying resources and reliable distribution of data and support the queries of greatest importance in our applications. This is accomplished by following the golden rule: NoSQL data models should be informed by the application's access patterns. A bad NoSQL design will be expensive, slow, and difficult to query. This chapter will explain how to approach data modeling in Azure Cosmos DB.

Introduction to Data Storage in Azure Cosmos DB

An important place to start is understanding how data is stored in Azure Cosmos DB. *JavaScript Object Notation* (JSON) is a popular file format for NoSQL databases. We will assume you are familiar with JSON, but if you are not, it is a self-describing, text-based format that looks like this:

© Steve Flowers 2023
S. Flowers, *Designing and Implementing Cloud-native Applications Using Microsoft Azure Cosmos DB*, Certification Study Companion Series, https://doi.org/10.1007/978-1-4842-9547-2_2

```
{
    "id": "e41e37fb-eaf6-4dd8-8eab-cf536e220837",
    "Name": "Blanca Quenneville",
    "Email": "Blanca.Quenneville@contoso.com",
    "Skills": ["Azure Cosmos DB", "Data", "Development"]
}
```

As you can see, integers, strings, and arrays (as well as additional data types) are supported, and they are self-describing in that when the preceding document is *deserialized*, it will represent the object and the data types of that object. JSON is stored in documents, and these documents are stored on nodes (i.e., servers) in Azure Cosmos DB.

Azure Cosmos DB leverages a *scale-out* architecture which means that in lieu of scaling nodes up by adding more CPU, more RAM, or more IOPS, the service scales out by adding more nodes. The idea of scale-out architecture explains a lot as to why Azure Cosmos DB behaves the way it does, and why data modeling is so important. Think of it like a bookshelf in a library; there needs to exist a large enough bookshelf with enough shelves to store the books that the library offers. When the library acquires more books, perhaps they could add shelves to the existing bookshelf, but there is certainly a limit, the ceiling only goes so high! So instead of increasing the size of one bookshelf, the library chooses to add more bookshelves as they provide more books. This is the idea behind scale-up versus scale-out distributed data architecture. Instead of adding resources to a single server, Azure Cosmos DB provisions additional servers to scale out, effectively making *elasticity* limitless and only confined to the bounds of the data center instead of a single node.

Based on this distribution, you may be wondering how your data is distributed or *sharded*. Library bookshelves use the Dewey Decimal system; what system do NoSQL databases and Azure Cosmos DB use? The answer to that question is the *partition key*, also sometimes referred to as a *shard key*. The partition key (PK for short) tells Azure Cosmos DB how to distribute data across nodes as your workload scales. The PK also helps your queries get routed to the correct physical node. Azure Cosmos DB uses consistent, hash-based partitioning based on the PK. A good PK will have high cardinality for even distribution. Consider the ISBN number of a magazine publication. The ISBN number identifies a magazine but not each individual issue. In the case of our library, this would allow patrons to find a magazine where they may not know which specific issue they need. Partitioning efficiency stems from a proper data model and is discussed further in Chapter 4.

Design and Implement a Nonrelational Data Model for Azure Cosmos DB Core API

In the NoSQL world, we have documents instead of rows and *collections* or *containers* instead of tables. So, when you think about a traditional relational model, you probably imagine tables and columns with a *primary key* and sometimes a *foreign key*, as well as the relationships between tables. For instance, consider a **SalesOrder** table which has a *1:N* relationship to the **SalesOrderDetail** table which in turn has a *N:1* relationship with the **Product** table. How do we represent this many-to-many relationship in NoSQL? What do I use for primary key and foreign keys?

NoSQL data modeling focuses on denormalization which breaks many of the rules we have learned from the relational world. We will still maintain references to other documents in our containers at times, but we won't concern ourselves with data duplication. In JSON, we can also have multivalued properties where the value of the property is an array or a sub-JSON object. In this chapter, the aim is to show you how we model data in NoSQL while referencing our familiar counterparts in the relational world.

Storing Multiple Entity Types in the Same Container

Consider the **SalesOrderHeader**, **SalesOrderDetail**, and **Product** tables of the *Adventure Works* sample data set provided in Azure SQL DB. Figure 2-1 shows the entity relationship diagram (ERD) for these tables.

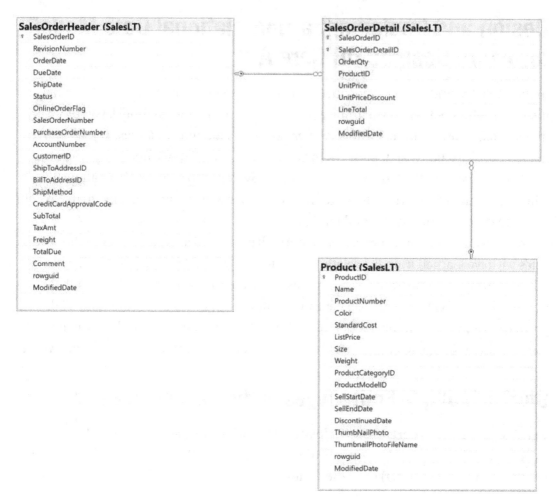

Figure 2-1. *Sales Order ERD*

As you can see in Figure 2-1, there is a *N:N* relationship between sales orders and products. This means many products can exist in many orders and many orders can contain many products. This is a common scenario for e-commerce applications. But how would we model this in Azure Cosmos DB? First, we do not want to create two different containers for these documents. Documents that are often queried together should reside in the same container. This is more efficient, and it allows us to serve multiple, related documents (entity types) from the same partition. Let's explore how we would model this in NoSQL and explain the benefits.

A user who would like to view their recent order from Adventure Works would likely open a page listing their recent orders. On this page, we wouldn't want to show every product in every order, rather a summary of the orders, the date they were placed, and their status. When the user clicks on a specific order, they expect to be able to view a list of products included in that order. Listings 2-1 and 2-2 show how we should design our data model.

Listing 2-1. Sales Order Document

```
{
    "id" : 123,
    "doctype" : "order",
    "revisionNumber" : 3,
    "orderDate" : "2022/08/06 04:00:00",
    "dueDate" : "2022/08/12 04:00:00",
    "shipDate" : "",
    "status" : "pending",
    "Product" : [
        {
            "id" : 101,
            "name" : "widget1",
            "quantity" : 3
        },
        {
            "id" : 105,
            "name" : "widget7",
            "quantity" : 1
        }
    ],
    Additional properties omitted...
}
```

Listing 2-2. Product Document

```
{
    "id" : 101,
    "doctype" : "product",
    "name" : "widget1",
    "standardCost" : "3.99",
    "listPrice" : "5.99",
    "weight" : "0.25",
    Additional properties omitted...

}
```

Since these documents will often be queried together, they should be collocated in the same container. We implement the "doctype" property to allow us to query the documents we need, and partition documents. A user viewing an order on the Adventure Works web page will be able to see a summary of their order easily and be able to click through a product link and pull up information on that product. We have *embedded* a summary of the product in the Sales Order document.

Storing Multiple Related Entities in the Same Document

The flexibility of JSON allows us to embed data in our documents, reference data in other documents, and implement a hybrid approach of both. The preceding Sales Order document is an example of the hybrid approach. There are prerequisites you should keep in mind when determining which approach to implement. When determining if you should take the embed approach, consider if the data model requires

- Contained relationships

- One-to-few relationships

- Infrequent change

- Queried together

- Bounded growth

When considering the reference approach, consider if the data model requires

- One-to-many relationships

- Many-to-many relationships

- Unbounded growth

And finally, when considering the hybrid approach, consider if the data model requires

- Improved read performance for most accessed data

- Aggregates

- Flexible read and write access

Figure 2-2 is a visual representation of the three approaches. The embed approach represents all data contained in a single document. The reference approach represents a schema where what would be one document in the embed approach broken out into multiple documents. And the hybrid approach represents some data that is embedded and the rest is referenced.

Figure 2-2. *Embed, Reference, Hybrid*

As you can see, embedding is beneficial for a bounded set of information, and by embedding it, read performance is increased. Azure Cosmos DB will retrieve data from a single document faster than it will by retrieving multiple documents. The improved read performance translates into lower query cost and lower latency. However, there are many trade-offs to consider in the NoSQL world. Larger documents are more expensive to write and even more expensive to update. In the case of the Sales Orders document, if we embedded all the information into a single document using an array of JSON objects, the document would become more and more expensive to update as new items are added to the order. This is not scalable.

The reference method splits the data into multiple documents. This data would normally be represented as an array. Reading becomes more expensive as the service must find more documents, but writing is improved since the document size has been reduced by including less information. This is most appropriate when considering an array that could grow rather large, and no upper bound exists to the total number of objects. In our example, we create a reference to the full Product document by embedding the Product ID into the Sales Order document.

The hybrid approach attempts to hedge the trade-offs of the other two approaches. Using our Sales Order data as an example, the hybrid approach allows us to see a summary of the products in our order which is read performant while also reducing the document size by not storing all of the product data. A trade-off is introduced in this pattern however, and it is due to denormalization. If you reference a subset of a product's properties in the SalesOrder document, what happens if the name of a product is updated? We must implement a mechanism to maintain the reference. This can easily be done using the *change feed* which will be discussed in a later chapter. But think of the change feed as akin to a change data capture (CDC) table on a SQL server. Using the change feed, we can trigger an update to all references based on the update of the product document.

The hybrid approach illustrates how we can develop a model that denormalizes data across documents. This is an important diversion from the rules we abide by in the relational world. This provides greater flexibility for a design which optimizes performance and reduces latency to accommodate the way we access our data. The idea of data denormalization is a topic that will surely be present in the case studies of the exam.

Document Features and Constraints

Azure Cosmos DB and NoSQL in general implement a primary key via the "id" property. This property must exist on every document, is unique, and as such uniquely identifies each document in the container. The "id" field must be unique within a logical partition, be a string, and not exceed the 255 character limit. The combination of the ID and the partition key provides the *index* of a document which helps Azure Cosmos DB know exactly where to find a specific document.

We can also apply the unique constraint to other properties in our document by defining unique keys when creating a container. Figure 2-3 displays the input box which allows us to define the path to our unique keys.

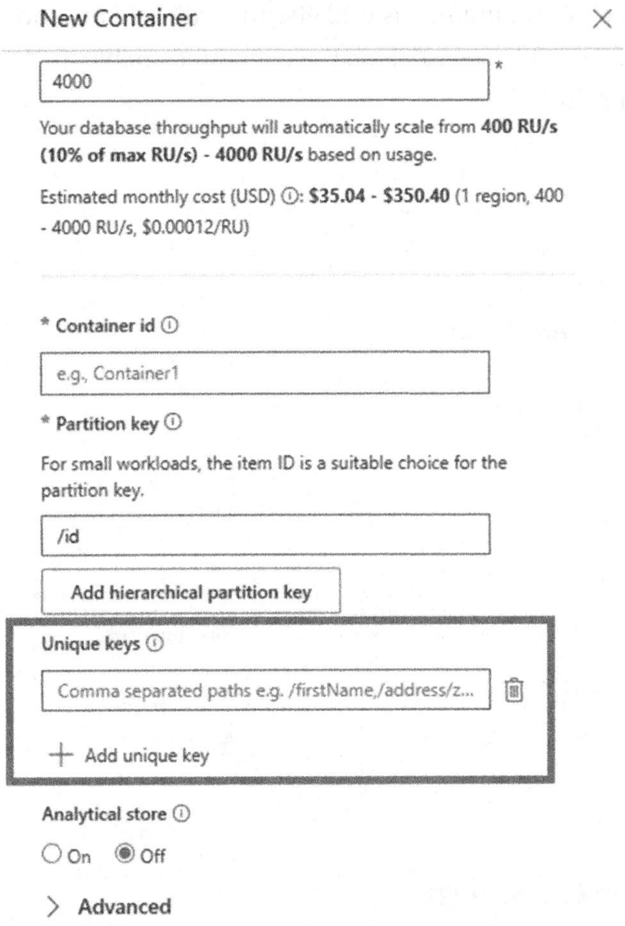

New Container   ✕

4000   *

Your database throughput will automatically scale from **400 RU/s**
(10% of max RU/s) - **4000 RU/s** based on usage.

Estimated monthly cost (USD) ⓘ: **$35.04** - **$350.40** (1 region, 400
- 4000 RU/s, $0.00012/RU)

* Container id ⓘ

e.g., Container1

* Partition key ⓘ

For small workloads, the item ID is a suitable choice for the
partition key.

/id

Add hierarchical partition key

Unique keys ⓘ

Comma separated paths e.g. /firstName,/address/z...   🗑

+ Add unique key

Analytical store ⓘ

○ On   ⦿ Off

〉 Advanced

Figure 2-3. *Add Unique Keys*

By adding properties to this field, Azure Cosmos DB will enforce uniqueness within
a logical partition. Consider our Products logical partition where products have an ID
and a name. The ID will already be constrained as unique but suppose we also want
to ensure the names of our products are unique. When we create the container to
store these documents, we can define the constraint by adding "/name" in the unique
keys field.

Another feature that is useful to know and important to understand for the exam is
time-to-live (*TTL*). TTL defines a time in seconds which will delete documents based
on the "_ts" property. The "_ts" property stands for *timestamp* and represents the last
modified time of a document based on *epoch time* in seconds. TTL can be configured at
the container level or on individual documents. To leverage document-level TTL, TTL

must be configured on the container as well else the "ttl" field on a document will be ignored. If you do not want to set a TTL on the container, enable the feature and set the option to "On (no default)."

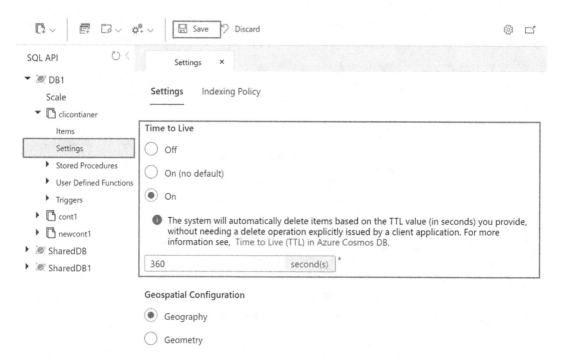

Figure 2-4. *Time to Live Settings*

When setting TTL on a container or document, you can set the value to "-1" to signify that the container should not expire documents (on, no default) or that the document should not expire. If you set the TTL at the container level, any document which does not have a "ttl" property will honor the container-level TTL. Listing 2-3 demonstrates setting the TTL at the container level using the C# SDK.

Listing 2-3. Setting TTL at the Container Level

```
Database database = client.GetDatabase("database");

ContainerProperties properties = new ()
{
    Id = "container",
    PartitionKeyPath = "/customerId",
```

```
    // Expire all documents after 90 days
    DefaultTimeToLive = 90 * 60 * 60 * 24
};

// Create a new container with TTL enabled and without any expiration value
Container container = await database
    .CreateContainerAsync(properties);
```

TTL set at the document level will take precedence over TTL set at the container level. Listing 2-4 demonstrates how to set the TTL at the container level.

Listing 2-4. Set the TTL on a Document

```
public record SalesOrder(string id, string customerId, int? ttl);

Container container = database.GetContainer("container");

SalesOrder item = new (
    "SO05",
    "CO18009186470"
    // Expire sales order in 30 days using "ttl" property
    ttl:  60 * 60 * 24 * 30
);

await container.CreateItemAsync<SalesOrder>(item);
```

Summary

Data modeling is an important subject to understand in the world of NoSQL. It is a fundamental skill to properly implement NoSQL workloads on Azure Cosmos DB as well as understand the questions and use cases presented on the exam. Unlike the relational world, we can use the flexibility of JSON documents to meet the performance and latency needs of our application. Each decision comes with trade-offs which makes careful planning important.

CHAPTER 3

Plan and Implement Sizing and Scaling

Azure Cosmos DB leverages scale-out architecture to meet high-demand workloads at global scale. This means that new nodes are added to the pool of resources instead of increasing the size of a single node. This is important to understand as this scaling determines how to choose the right PK and what limits exist within a distributed, scale-out architecture.

In this chapter we will introduce concepts such as *logical* and *physical* partitions, how they affect your workload, and how Azure Cosmos DB assigns and provides throughput to your workload. These are important topics, not only for the test, but for your production workloads. These limits and trade-offs must be addressed in the design stage of your application to ensure your Azure Cosmos DB implementation is truly scalable.

Azure Cosmos DB Under the Hood

Let's look under the hood of Azure Cosmos DB and start by introducing the architecture behind the scenes of an account. This is an important topic as it helps solidify your partition key decisions and understanding of scale and performance. As discussed previously, Azure Cosmos DB is a scale-out service, which means additional nodes are added to the pool of resources to meet demand. Azure Cosmos DB is PaaS, which means you typically do not need to concern yourself with the inner workings of the architecture. But it is important to understand how this architecture impacts your workload. The way that these nodes or *throughput* are provisioned depends on the throughput provisioning model, of which, Azure Cosmos DB has three.

© Steve Flowers 2023
S. Flowers, *Designing and Implementing Cloud-native Applications Using Microsoft Azure Cosmos DB*, Certification Study Companion Series, https://doi.org/10.1007/978-1-4842-9547-2_3

An Azure Cosmos DB account is made up of three keys components: the account, the databases, and the containers. The account is the top-level resource you deploy into your Azure environment. This is where you will manage role-based access control (RBAC), firewall, and features and access the *Data Explorer*. The Data Explorer allows you to manage your databases, manage throughput, and issue queries against your containers. Databases are the next level of your Azure Cosmos DB resource. They will be comprised of your containers and can also be allocated throughput. Finally, your containers are the buckets that your data will be stored in and can also be allocated throughput. If we think back to the example of a library, the library itself is the account, rooms are the databases, and sections of the rooms are the containers. Finally, the granular control over how much processing we can perform on the data in our containers is defined by *request units*, or *RUs*. Allocating more RUs means we can store more data and more physical partitions are deployed. RUs represent the throughput available to our databases or containers.

The hierarchy of Azure Cosmos DB entities is pictured in Figure 3-1: the account at the highest level, then the databases within, and finally, the containers which reside within databases.

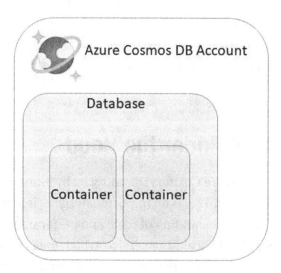

Figure 3-1. *Account Hierarchy*

It is important to understand this hierarchy, but this is all abstraction to what is really being deployed to the service under the hood. To understand sizing and scaling, we need to be familiar with the way in which Azure Cosmos DB provides throughput to our containers. As mentioned earlier, this impacts our performance and partitioning. There are two main ideas that are important to understand: these are *logical partitions* and *physical partitions.*

Logical partitions are the subsets of our data that are defined by our partitioning key. You will sometimes hear logical partitions referred to as *key ranges* since a logical partition is defined by our partition key, and a range of those keys will be assigned to each physical partition. For instance, if we partitioned by a customer's name in our e-commerce application, each customer would have a logical partition that comprises their data. This is again beneficial to scaling and performance as queries which need to read a specific customer's orders would only be routed to a single logical partition. If your application includes hundreds or thousands of customers, across tens or hundreds of physical partitions, the partition key and hence the identification of your logical partitions means that the query must only be routed to the specific physical partition that contains that specific customer's data. Notice I didn't say "partitions," plural. This was done purposefully because at this time, a logical partition can only be contained within a single physical partition. But more on that later.

Physical partitions are the physical resources that make up our cluster. When we think of a cluster, we must think of *nodes* in a cluster. As we increase our need to store data or serve requests, more nodes must be added. In Azure Cosmos DB, physical partitions are made up of four nodes. There is a leader node and three follower nodes, as shown in Figure 3-2. When using the *multi-write* capabilities of Azure Cosmos DB, one of the follower nodes will be designated a *forwarder* node, which is responsible for replicating data to other geographic regions. We also consider a physical partition to be a *replica set* because it is a load-balanced group of *replicas* spread across fault domains.

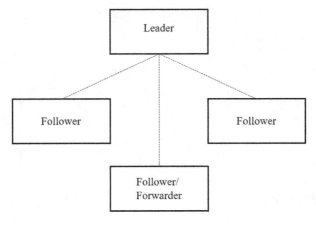

Figure 3-2. *Replica Sets*

In the case of a *multi-region* deployment, whether that be a multi-write deployment (allowing writes to more than one geographic region) or a *multi-read* deployment (allowing only read to be served from more than one geographic region), replica sets are replicated to each region that has been configured for the Azure Cosmos DB account. Since logical partitions are tied to a physical partition, when replica sets are replicated to additional regions, these paired replica sets become *partition sets*. Partition sets make up the replica sets that are replicated to different regions but contain the same logical partitions.

In Figure 3-3, there are two replica sets in the East US region and two in the West US region. The relationship between the replica set in East US and the replica set in West US is defined by the logical partitions that they share. The two leftmost replica sets are part of one partition set and the two rightmost are part of one partition set. In this case, a follower will be designated as a forwarder to replicate data between the two replica sets. If your account is configured for a multi-region deployment with only one write region, only the write region will have a forwarder. If implementing multi-write, then both replica sets in the partition set will have a forwarder.

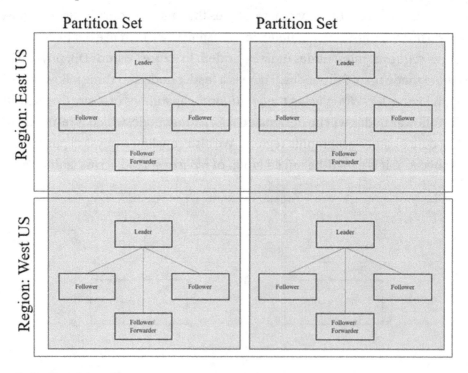

Figure 3-3. *Partition Sets*

Throughput Provisioning

Throughput provisioning is an important concept which will certainly be a topic of questions on the exam, as well as case studies. Throughput provisioning is defined by the number of request units (RUs) that we assign to our workloads. RUs are an abstraction of CPU, memory, and IOPS that provide a granular yet easy to understand mechanism for controlling performance as well as cost at scale. Our operations (reads, writes, updates, deletes) have an RU cost associated with them which will inform how many RUs we need provisioned to support the workload. RUs can be provisioned at the container level, or at the database level. RUs provisioned at the database level are considered *shared*, which will be discussed in the next section. There are three throughput provisioning models: *manual*, *autoscale*, and *serverless*.

Manual Provisioned Throughput

Manual provisioned throughput is the method of assigning a static number of RUs to your workload. The lowest number of RUs we can configure is 400, and the maximum is theoretically unlimited. If 1k RUs is configured, on an hour-by-hour basis, we will be billed for 1k RUs plus our storage cost. When leveraging manual provisioned throughput, it is important to first determine how many RUs are required for your workload. If we identify that at most 200 concurrent connections will be made to the database to read and write documents, and those reads and writes cost 5 RUs and 15 RUs, respectively, and furthermore that roughly 80% of the operations are reads and 20% of the operations are writes, we can determine the throughput needed to meet the demand of the workload.

> *200 users * .80 * 15 RUs = 2,400 RUs*

> *200 users * .20 * 5 RUs = 200 RUs*

To meet this workload, we need 2,600 RUs or else HTTP status code *429* errors will be returned. The 429 error indicates that the provisioned throughput has been exceeded. The client will attempt to retry based on the retry policy. A small percentage of 429s is acceptable (1–5%) as they will likely be mitigated by retries which are automatically configured in the connection when using the Azure Cosmos DB SDK. It is a good idea to leave some buffer in this case if an unexpected spike of traffic is received. There are new features in Azure Cosmos DB such as *bursting* to account for this, but this feature is outside of the scope of the exam at the time of this writing. In addition to the RU requirements for our operations, we also need provisioned RUs for the storage of our account. Ten RUs are required per 1 GB of data stored.

Manual provisioned throughput is best for workloads that may see small spikes in operations but overall are mostly flat. As you can see in Figure 3-4, throughout the day the RU consumption is mostly flat, but there is room in the provisioned RUs to accommodate small spikes. Manual provisioned throughput is best for workloads with predictable throughput requirements.

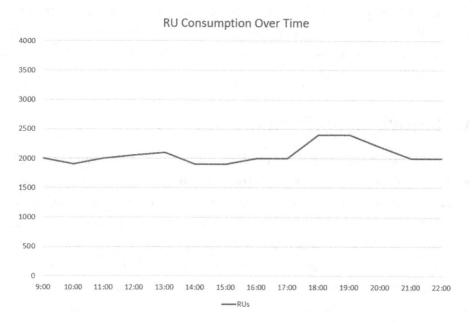

Figure 3-4. *Manual RU Consumption over Time*

When provisioning manual throughput, Azure Cosmos DB will use the number of RUs provisioned to determine how many physical partitions to create. When the number of RUs increases, more physical partitions will be created. When you initially create a container and provision RUs, one physical partition will be created for every 6,000 RUs.

> *3,000 RUs = 1 Physical Partition*
>
> *6,000 RUs = 1 Physical Partition*
>
> *7,000 RUs = 2 Physical Partitions*
>
> *13,000 RUS = 3 Physical Partitions*

When you have multiple physical partitions, RUs are split evenly across them. If we select to provision 9,000 RUs, two physical partitions will be created and be allotted 4,500 RUs each. After initial creation, when additional RUs are added, new physical partitions will be created for every 10k RUs. For example, I first create a container and assign 9k RUs. Two physical partitions of 4.5k RUs are created. I later increase my RUs to 14k, I will still have two physical partitions of 7k RUs each. If I again increase the RUs to 21k, I will now have a third physical partition created. Each physical partition will have 7k RUs. Figure 3-5 shows how throughput is split between partitions in the scenario described.

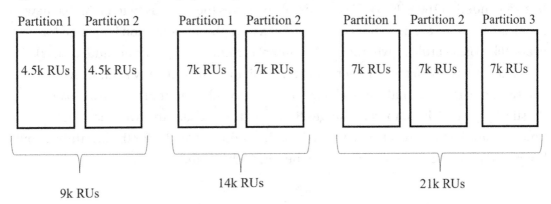

Figure 3-5. *Distributing Throughput Among Partitions*

Physical partitions have a max limit of 10k RUs, hence the need to add additional physical partitions when the RUs exceed this amount. Additionally, since a logical partition is tied to a single physical partition, the max number of RUs for a logical partition is also 10k.

Autoscale Provisioned Throughput

Autoscale provisioned throughput works in the exact same way as manual, except you can set the upper bounds of the RUs your workload needs, and Azure Cosmos DB will only bill you for the RUs you consume. It works the same as manual provisioned throughput behind the scenes, so think of it as a billing mechanism to help control costs. There are three important characteristics of autoscale that are important:

- Autoscale RUs cost 1.5x manual RUs.

- Autoscale has a minimum number of RUs: 10% of the maximum RUs.

- New physical partitions will be created on demand as autoscale requests more RUs while scaling.

Autoscale has an increased cost when compared to manual RUs. The increased cost comes from the fact that resources are reserved so that autoscale scales instantly when your workload demands additional RUs. Unlike other services, there is no wait time for cluster/node provisioning in the back end to provide the additional resources. Autoscale also has a minimum number of RUs you will be billed for. The best way to leverage autoscale is to set the minimum as close as possible to your baseline to ensure you are paying the minimum most of the time, and scaling to meet spikes in operations to prevent 429 errors. Previously, the min/max was 400 RUs/ 4k RUs. Recently this has been amended to 100 RUs/ 1k RUs. Autoscale operates the same as manual in that new physical partitions are provisioned except that a new physical partition is created for every 10k RUs regardless (whether that be initial creation or RUs that are added later).

Figure 3-6 shows a traffic pattern that is best fit for autoscale provisioning. As you can see, hour-by-hour traffic has a lot of spikes. Every other hour in this case is using drastically lower RUs. Autoscale charges RUs based on the max that were used in that hour, so based on Figure 3-6, you would be billed around 400 RUs for the low throughput hours and around 2k–2.5k RUs for the higher throughput hours.

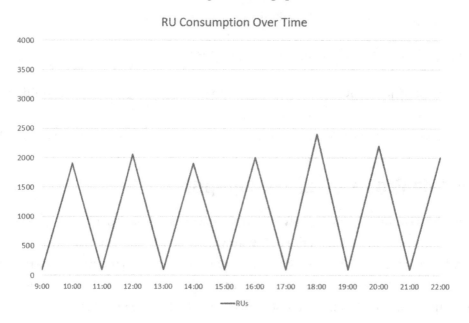

Figure 3-6. *Autoscale RU Consumption over Time*

Serverless Throughput

Serverless throughput is not considered "provisioned" since the resources are not dedicated to your workload. Serverless is considered a "consumption-based offering" as you are only billed for the RUs that you consume. It is important to note here, however, that you are billed for storage in Azure Cosmos DB as well as RUs. The consumption-based nature of serverless provides straightforward pricing with no overhead as RUs are consumed on a per-query basis. You do not have to commit to a specific amount of RUs and there is no additional cost when not using the serverless throughput.

Serverless is a great throughput model when you are just getting started with Azure Cosmos DB or working with development workloads. It can be appropriate for some production workloads but there are some limitations to serverless throughput. A serverless account can only run in a single region. By using serverless, you no longer gain the benefit and scale of a multi-region deployment. Additionally, serverless containers can only store a maximum of 50 GB (however, at this time 1 TB of storage is currently in preview). Serverless-provisioned containers are also limited to a single physical partition, hence the lack of multi-region support. The limitation of a single physical partition limits your serverless throughput per container to 5k RUs. Even though the max RU per physical container is 10k RUs, the limit on serverless containers remains 5k RUs. The consumption pattern of a container that would benefit from serverless would look like Figure 3-7.

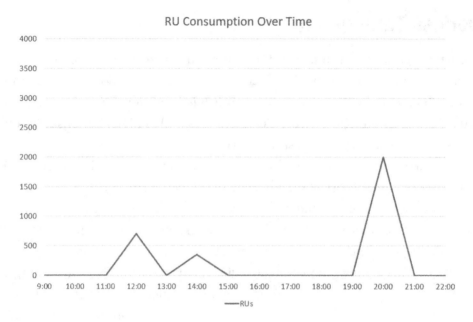

Figure 3-7. *Serverless RU Consumption over Time*

Shared Throughput Provisioning

As mentioned in the previous section, there are two methods of provisioning: *dedicated* and *shared*. Dedicated throughput is the process of defining the amount of RUs provisioned at the container level. When using dedicated throughput, each container has its own RUs and will not be affected by the throughput of other containers, also known as *noisy neighbors*. This type of provisioning ensures your containers have the RUs they require without disruption, but there is typically overhead. As mentioned earlier, when using manual throughput, it is good to have a 15–20% buffer to accommodate spikes. But over many containers this is a lot of wasted resources. Shared provisioning allows you to determine the total number of RUs at the database level and define containers which will share that throughput.

When you first create a database, the database creation wizard will provide you with the option to provision throughput for the database. Doing so will create shared throughput that child containers of that database can leverage. By not provisioning throughput, you are forcing a dedicated throughput pattern as child containers must provision their own throughput. Once you have provisioned throughput for a database, the throughput cannot be removed, only modified. To summarize, checking the "provision throughput" check box in the new database creation wizard will configure your database for shared throughput. Unchecking the box will require that child containers of the database have dedicated throughput. Figure 3-8 is an example of what the new database screen looks like in the Azure Portal.

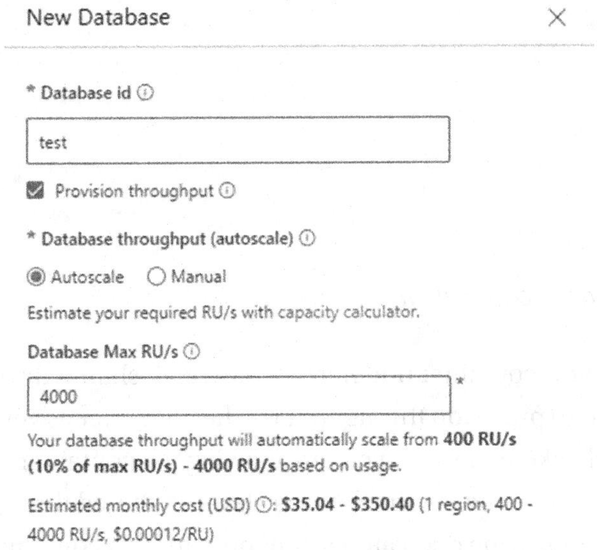

Figure 3-8. *Database Creation Wizard Throughput Provisioning*

Databases with provisioned throughput will have a "Scale" tab which allows modification of the throughput provisioned at the database level as you can see in Figure 3-9 when looking at the "shared" database.

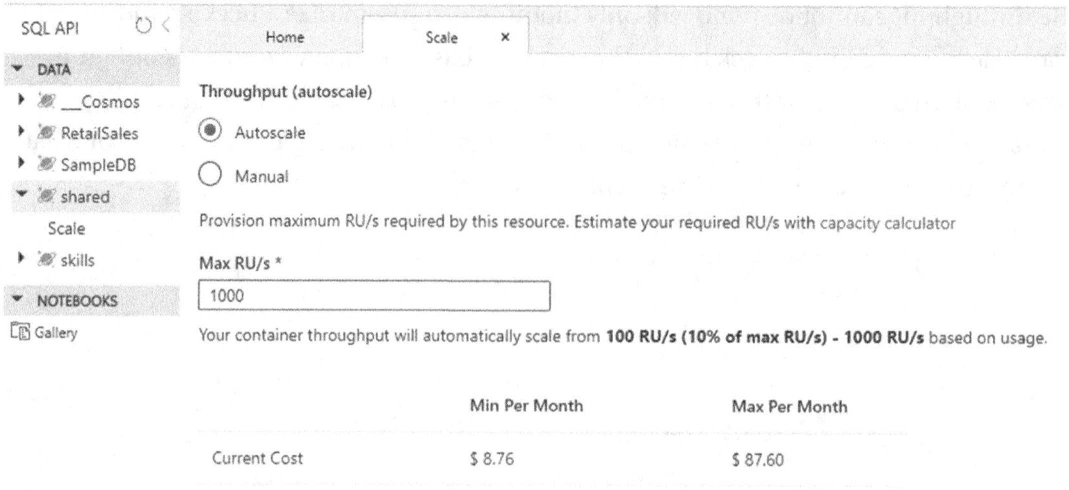

Figure 3-9. Database Scale Settings

When creating a new container under a database with shared throughput, you are offered the option to provision throughput for the container as you can see in Figure 3-10. By **not** checking this box, you are allowing the container to leverage the throughput that was provisioned at the database level as shared throughput. If this box is checked, you are configuring dedicated throughput for this container that will not consume the shared throughput of the database. As you can see, dedicated and shared containers can both coexist in the same database and there is granular control over which containers have dedicated throughput and which are using shared throughput.

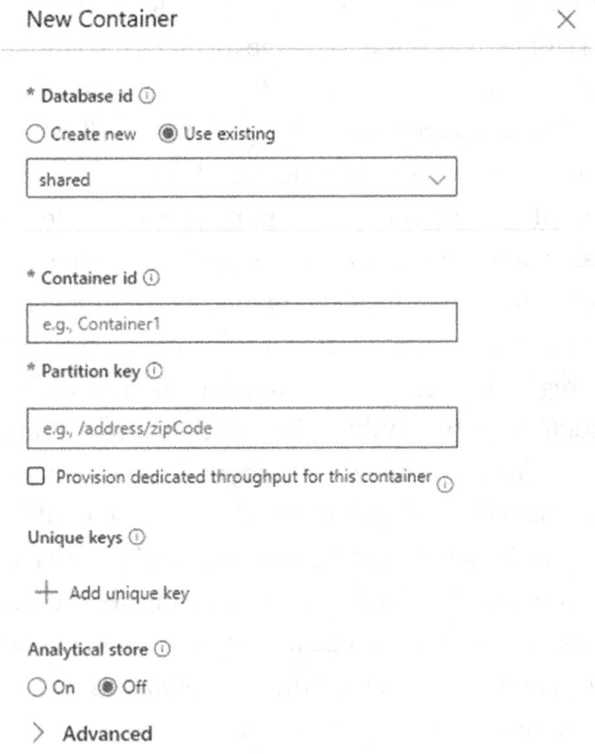

New Container   ✕

* Database id ⓘ
○ Create new   ⦿ Use existing

shared   ⌄

* Container id ⓘ

e.g., Container1

* Partition key ⓘ

e.g., /address/zipCode

☐ Provision dedicated throughput for this container ⓘ

Unique keys ⓘ

+ Add unique key

Analytical store ⓘ
○ On   ⦿ Off

〉 Advanced

Figure 3-10. New Container Throughput Provisioning

In my experience it is common to mix both dedicated and shared throughput in the same database. The shared throughput can be used for the lesser used containers which may not require as much throughput, and the dedicated containers can be allocated with their own RUs to serve the most important, high-demand queries in the application. Shared throughput is often commonly seen across *multi-tenant* applications as some tenants may be busier than others. There is a limitation to be aware of though, shared throughput can only be shared across a maximum of 25 containers. Beyond the 25 containers, dedicated throughput containers can still be created in the database.

Plan and Manage Cost

Request units are a granular cost metric that allow you to plan for your resource consumption at scale. RUs provide a very straightforward way for admins to control costs and understand the cost impact of specific queries, rather than estimating CPU,

RAM, and IOPS. Azure Cosmos DB's pricing model includes the cost of RUs as well as the cost of consumed storage. Consumed storage includes the amount of data you are storing in your account which includes storage for backups. Links have been provided in the companion GitHub for Azure Cosmos DB pricing as well as a capacity calculator. The capacity calculator allows you to input the size of your documents, the types of operations, and the number of regions to determine your estimated monthly spend.

Adding additional regions multiplies your Azure Cosmos DB cost by the number of regions. Single-region write accounts with N number of additional read regions will cost N times the number of RUs of the write region. For example, if you have a write region in East US and a read region in West US, and your container is configured for 4k RUs, you will be charged for 8k RUs. In a multi-write scenario, the costs are increased for the base price of RUs. In manual provisioned throughput, RUs cost \$0.008/hour/100 RUs. When you create a second write region in West US, the base cost of RUs increases to \$0.016/hour/100 RUs. The benefit is that if one of your regions fails, your workload can resume in another region. The drawback is you are paying double for your RUs. However, additional read regions can be used for read operations, just make sure there are enough RUs to accommodate your workload if the primary region fails and the secondary region needs to handle the addition read/write workload.

Cost Management in the Azure Portal can be used like most other services to monitor the cost of your accounts, set budgets and alerts, and so on. Additionally, the Cost Management pane in the Azure Portal for an Azure Cosmos DB account supports setting a "total throughput limit." Enabling this feature allows admins to set the ceiling on how many RUs can be provisioned within the account. Azure Cosmos DB has massive scale, and this setting can ensure that developers who need additional throughput cannot increase beyond the allotted threshold without speaking to the business. See Figure 3-11, which shows the screen for limiting throughput on an account.

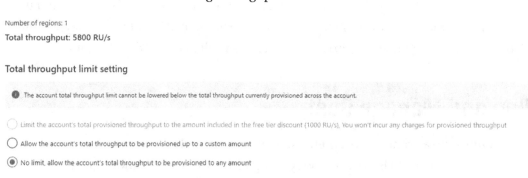

Figure 3-11. *Azure Cosmos DB Cost Management Throughput Limits*

Summary

Understanding sizing and scaling is an important aspect of your Azure Cosmos DB workloads. Choosing the correct throughput model will ensure your application can scale. Also understanding how this scale occurs is important for cost optimization and performance optimization. Many times excessive cost comes from poorly written queries or an improperly defined data model. Having a firm grasp of these concepts will lead to successful deployment of your applications leveraging Azure Cosmos DB. The DP-420 exam will also expect you to have a strong grasp of these concepts.

CHAPTER 4

Design a Data Partitioning Strategy

In distributed data systems, the way we partition the data among the physical resources is considered a *partitioning strategy*. Unlike *monolithic* data systems, distributed data systems distribute data between the physical nodes available to our cluster. By distributing data in this way, it is possible to spend less resources to query specific data quickly from a single node or use the power of the distributed nodes to allow us to query a lot of data extremely fast. Our partitioning strategy helps us find the right partition key for the most efficient use of resources.

The partition key determines how to distribute the data among the available nodes. As mentioned in the last chapter, a logical partition will be tied to a single physical node. If we distribute data based on customer name, for example, a logical partition will be created for each value of customer name. The logical partitions are distributed evenly across our physical partitions based on a hashed value of the partition key. If Customer A queries their data, the query will be routed only to the physical partition with their data. If a client issues a query which includes all customers, the power of the distributed physical partitions will ensure the results are returned quickly. In this chapter, I will cover how to choose a partitioning strategy, choosing a partition key, and evaluating the cost of data partitioning.

Choose a Partitioning Strategy

Let's start the discussion of partitioning strategy with an example use case. You are a developer responsible for an e-commerce application that hosts products for thousands of vendors. Vendors are constantly adding new products, removing old products, and updating existing products. Users of the application are browsing products, adding them

© Steve Flowers 2023
S. Flowers, *Designing and Implementing Cloud-native Applications Using Microsoft Azure Cosmos DB*, Certification Study Companion Series, https://doi.org/10.1007/978-1-4842-9547-2_4

to their cart, and tracking the status of their order. In the second chapter, we discussed data modeling and the golden rule: store your data in the way in which it is accessed. To begin to understand the correct data strategy, first understand the workload access patterns. Understanding the partitioning strategy helps us decide what the appropriate partition key should be.

Vendors of the e-commerce site could have tens, hundreds, or thousands of products. They likely browse their catalog of products and make updates, add new products, and delete discontinued items. For the sake of this example, let's say vendors only care about their products and don't own/manage multiple vendors. For vendors, it is likely best to create a container where the partition key is a property like "vendor_id" (not to be confused with the more generic "ID" property). It could be a generated unique ID like a UUID, or a plain text string. The document would look like Listing 4-1.

Listing 4-1. Example Vendor Document

```
{
    "id" : "66f20982-74a4-44b0-94c9-e8c7b7cebb86",
    "vendor_id" : "buyberriesonline.com",
    "vendor_location" : "California",
    "vendor_description" : "Online wholesale provider of widgets."
    Additional properties omitted...

}
```

The value of this property now determines which documents share the same logical partition. Queries which include the "vendor_id" will be routed to the single physical partition where the vendor's documents are stored. Be careful of a common mistake, however. The partition key cannot be edited and the only way to change it is to rewrite the document. Text string for vendor ID could be problematic if you need to update it later. If "vendor_id" is set to the name of the vendor such as "buyberriesonline.com" and later the name of the company changes, the documents would need to be rewritten.

When a vendor uses our e-commerce application to query their own products, their query will be routed to a single physical partition that contains the logical partition which represents their vendor ID. A query which would target the specific logical partition of a vendor would include the "vendor_id" value in a WHERE clause like the following:

```
SELECT * FROM c WHERE c.vendor_id = "buyberriesonline.com"
```

Without the WHERE clause, the query wouldn't know which vendor the query was targeting and therefore does not have the information necessary to route the query to a single partition. A query that does not include the partition key in a WHERE clause will be routed to all physical partitions. This is called a *cross-partition* query also known as a *fan-out* query. Cross-partition queries are the most expensive from a RU perspective as well as a latency perspective. Cross-partition queries are not optimal, but they cannot always be avoided. The aim is to limit our cross-partition queries to the least percentage of queries while optimizing the most common queries with our partitioning strategy.

Users of the e-commerce application will likely be interacting with many vendors as they browse the site, view different products, and add products to their shopping cart. Users would be created in a new partition and be partitioned by a unique user ID and their user document would include name, address, payment profile, and email address. In a user's logical partition, you would likely store documents related to their shopping cart, order history, preferences, and so on. As mentioned in Chapter 2, it would probably be best to take a hybrid approach and store a document in the user's container with the user's ID and a summary of their cart instead of querying the vendor container to view their cart. The documents would look like in Listings 4-2 and 4-3. The first document is the user's document and the second is the user's cart document.

Listing 4-2. User Document

```
{
    "id" : "876538f6-38af-4026-8ec5-ded2140ea6e2",
    "user_id" : "876538f6-38af-4026-8ec5-ded2140ea6e2",
    "doc_type" : "user"
    "user_name" : "Joey Lamb",
    "user_email" : "jlambLovesBerries224@outlook.com",
    Additional properties omitted...
}
```

Listing 4-3. User Cart Document

```
{
    "id" : "839cd4b3-0785-4868-9ec3-e8a12b4b2519",
    "user_id" : "876538f6-38af-4026-8ec5-ded2140ea6e2",
    "doc_type" : "user_cart",
    "user_cart" : [
```

```
    {
        "item_id" : "1c42d3a1-e9ab-456d-85b4-4441c929044f",
        "item_name" : "Chocolate Coverd Strawberries",
        "quantity" : 3
    },
    {
        "item_id" : "cda25e5c-7b3f-4181-91f9-ddb49dea5443",
        "item_name" : "Pineapple",
        "quantity" : 1
    }
    ]
    Additional properties omitted...
}
```

As you can see from Listing 4-2, we included a property called "doc_type" which helps us identify what kind of document we are querying while still partitioning on the "user_id" property. All queries which include the "user_id" will be routed to a single physical partition.

Choose a Partition Key

Choosing the right partition key properly distributes your data across physical partitions. Azure Cosmos DB will automatically partition your data based on the value of the partition key you have selected. The first important consideration is the *data model* that you are implementing and the properties that will make up that data model. In the case of the e-commerce application, vendors will have a vendor ID, vendor name, vendor URL, and so on. Determine which of these would be a suitable candidate for a partition key by following these basic rules: a partition key must ensure high *cardinality* of the data, be *immutable*, and a value we know. The last rule of a "value we know" is due to the fact that we must know the value in order to include it in our WHERE clause. There are ways to mitigate this using Azure Cognitive Search, but that is outside of the scope of this book.

The partition key is chosen during the container creation step and should be a string or an integer. Figure 4-1 demonstrates the experience in the portal. The partition key value requires the path to the property you have chosen.

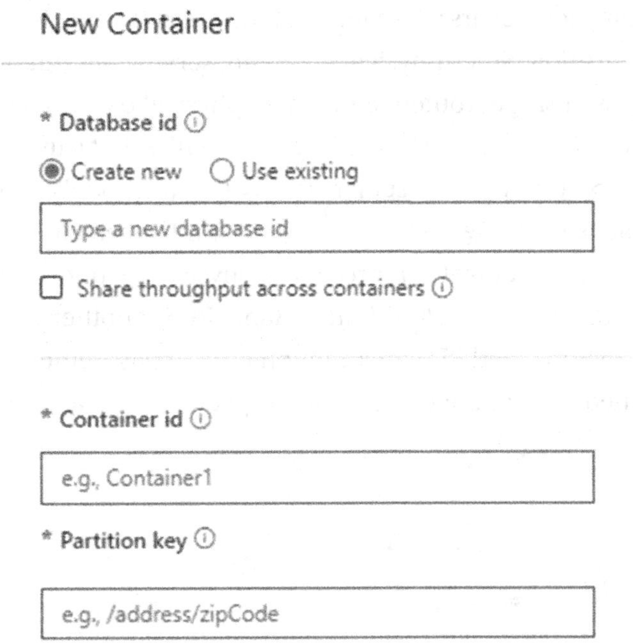

New Container

* Database id ⓘ

◉ Create new   ◯ Use existing

Type a new database id

☐ Share throughput across containers ⓘ

* Container id ⓘ

e.g., Container1

* Partition key ⓘ

e.g., /address/zipCode

Figure 4-1. *New Container Partition Key*

Data cardinality in relation to the physical partitions ensures that queries can be routed to an individual physical partition when needed and leverage the entire cluster when performing cross-partition queries for high performance. High cardinality ensures data is evenly split among the physical partitions. To achieve high cardinality, a partition key with high cardinality must be chosen. If we consider the example of our e-commerce application, there are many users of the application and therefore partitioning by their user ID or email address would provide high cardinality. I would also ensure queries reading a specific customer's order are only routed to the physical partition that customer resides on. There can be a problem where your partition key creates too high a degree of cardinality. Imagine an IoT application producing time-series telemetry data containing the temperature measurements for a piece of machinery. If you would like to query a specific timeframe to understand if the machine is operating out of specifications, you would probably want to partition by the datetime produced by the machine. If the datetime stamp includes milliseconds, you will have many partitions and queries against multiple partitions will result in cross-partition queries.

Partitioning by timestamp in the IoT example could also create too much cardinality where you are querying too often against a single partition. This effect is referred to as a *hot partition.* A hot partition is the opposite of too much cardinality and reflects too little cardinality. A hot partition occurs when many of the queries being issued are routed to the same physical partition. Since physical nodes are serving our queries, when many of our queries continuously get routed to the same physical partition, that partition may become overworked due to the limited amount of RUs that can be served from a single partition. Hot partitions are a regular issue with data models and can be identified using the *Insights* blade of the Azure Cosmos DB account as seen in Figures 4-2 and 4-3. In Figure 4-3, "PartitionKeyRangeId" represents a physical partition which is at 100% utilization. As mentioned earlier, "PartitionKeyRangeId" is another way of identifying a partition key range. Normalized RU consumption is the measurement of the maximum throughput consumed over a period of time for a specific physical partition.

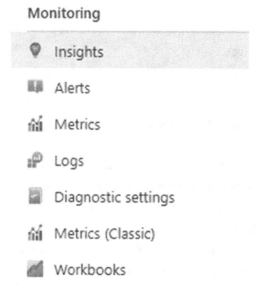

Figure 4-2. *Insights Blade in Azure Portal*

Normalized RU Consumption (Max) Heat Map By PartitionKeyRangeID - Database: RetailSales , Container: surfaceSales

Segment Field	↑↓	Throughput (RU)	↑↓	Timeline
∨ partitionkeyrangeid (5)				
0		100%		
3		1%		
2		0%		
1		0%		

Figure 4-3. *Hot Partition*

Sometimes it is difficult to determine the correct partition key based on the lack of a good candidate key. For instance, let's assume we have onboarded a new vendor who has millions of products. The documents representing the products would exceed the 20GB limit of a logical partition. There are also scenarios where we are not exceeding limits but the lack of cardinality based on our partition key choice is making our cross-partition queries slow. And finally, how do we fix data models that have too high a degree of cardinality? In these cases we can implement a *synthetic key*. A synthetic key is combining two pieces of data together to produce a new key which will solve our cardinality issues. If we think about the IoT scenario discussed earlier, there is too much cardinality if we partition on time when milliseconds are used in the timestamp. We could improve the distribution and queries by keeping the timestamp its own property but adding a new property called "pk" which summarizes the time and the machine. This improves our queries as well because we can ensure that queries for a specific IoT device are routed to a specific logical partition. The data model would look like Listing 4-4.

Listing 4-4. IoT Model with Synthetic Key

```
{
    "id" : "0ab4cbb5-3dd2-4b53-912c-283b21e01b8f",
    "pk" : "infraredScanner01_2022-09-07T13:35:08.4780000Z",
    "measure" : "0.01",
    "timestamp" : "2022-09-07T13:35:08.4780000Z"
    Additional properties omitted...
}
```

Evaluate the Cost of Data Partitioning

To evaluate the cost of our data partitioning, we will look at some example queries and the *Query Stats* that are provided in the Azure Cosmos DB Data Explorer. I will use an example data set of retail sales for Microsoft Surface devices. The data model for the documents in the container looks like Listing 4-5.

Listing 4-5. Sample Retail Sales Data Set

```
{
    "storeId": "70",
    "productCode": "surface.laptop3",
    "quantity": "156",
    "logQuantity": "9.656051309",
    "advertising": "1",
    "price": "279",
    "weekStarting": "9/26/2019",
    "id": "4015986d-7a55-4339-98e8-89120b4e84af"
    Additional properties omitted...
}
```

Our container is currently configured for 30k RUs which means we have three physical partitions. The partition key is "/storeId" and each "storeId" has its own logical partition on our cluster of three physical partitions. If I issue a query like SELECT * FROM c, I can view the *Request Charge* of the query in the Query Stats window below the query pane as seen in Figure 4-4.

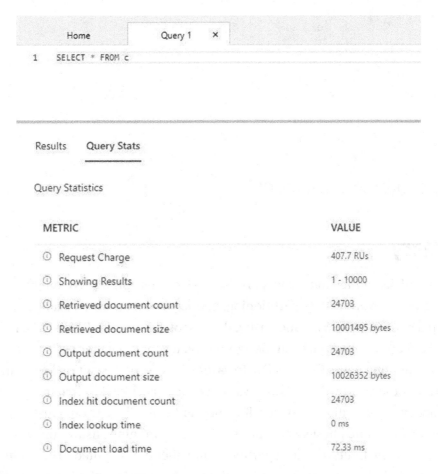

Figure 4-4. *Data Explorer Query Stats*

We can access additional information as to which physical partitions were involved in the query by clicking the "Per-partition query metrics (CSV)" link at the bottom of the Query Stats pane. The output of this file shows we issued the query against all three physical partitions and the query cost was 407.7 RUs.

If we alter the query to target a specific store, we will see how proper partitioning provides query optimization. After issuing the query `SELECT * FROM c WHERE c.storeId = "70"`, we can see the RU cost is significantly lower at 13.53 RUs and the per-partition query metrics shows only one of the physical partitions returned documents. The Query Stats are shown in Figure 4-5.

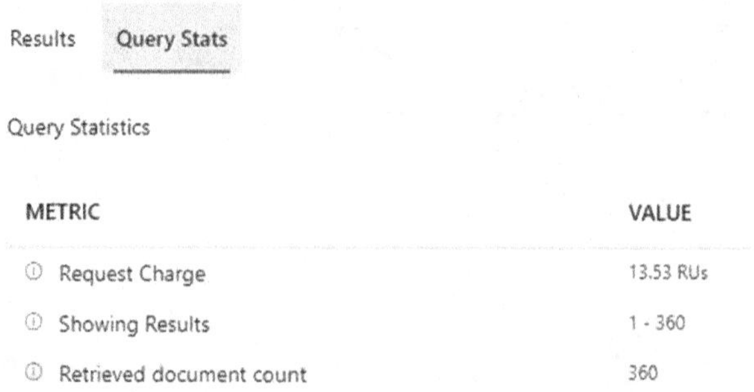

Results   **Query Stats**

Query Statistics

METRIC	VALUE
ⓘ Request Charge	13.53 RUs
ⓘ Showing Results	1 - 360
ⓘ Retrieved document count	360

Figure 4-5. *Query Stats WHERE Clause*

Summary

In the world of distributed data, data partitioning helps us optimize for our most common queries. Without data partitioning, queries would be issued against every physical partition in our cluster increasing the cost of our queries. Finding the right partition key can be a challenge, but designing and testing a data model is an important first step to adopting Azure Cosmos DB. In cases where a good partition key cannot be found, synthetic keys provide a flexible way to create a partition key that makes sense for our application. Partitions provide efficiency and scalability. As our clusters grow to include more and more physical partitions, proper partitioning ensures that our data does not exceed the limits of logical partitions and queries are routed to individual partitions instead of the entire cluster. This distribution and partitioning is how Azure Cosmos DB provides massive, global scale.

## CHAPTER 5

Implement Client Connectivity Options

Azure Cosmos DB is a multimodal database, which means there are multiple APIs surfaced by the service for developers to interact with. There is the Core (SQL) API, API for MongoDB, API for Cassandra, API for Gremlin, API for Azure Storage Tables, and the newest API for PostgreSQL. These APIs provide flexibility for developers who want to leverage a key/value store, document store, column-family, or graph. The multimodal nature of Azure Cosmos DB also makes migrating beneficial for developers looking to take advantage of the scalable, globally distributed nature of Azure Cosmos DB.

In this chapter we will cover creating a connection to an Azure Cosmos DB database using C#. Examples in this book will leverage C#, though Azure Cosmos DB supports .NET, .NET Core, Node.js, Java, Spring, Spark, Python, Go, SQL, and REST. Understanding how to implement a client and the connectivity options available through the SDK is an important objective for the exam. We will cover how to choose the correct connectivity mode, logging from the SDK, and using the Azure Cosmos DB Emulator for local development.

Working with the Azure Cosmos DB .NET SDK

There are currently two versions of the .NET SDK: version 2 and version 3. For this book, we will be using v3. To follow along in this section, make sure you have created an Azure Cosmos DB account and a new .NET project using your favorite IDE. Include the *Microsoft.Azure.Cosmos* package in your project to access the classes required to build a client and interact with your data store. We will be leveraging the Core API moving forward.

© Steve Flowers 2023
S. Flowers, *Designing and Implementing Cloud-native Applications Using Microsoft Azure Cosmos DB*, Certification Study Companion Series, https://doi.org/10.1007/978-1-4842-9547-2_5

There are several properties we need from our Azure Cosmos DB account to connect using the SDK. To start we need the *endpoint URI* and the *primary key* which can be retrieved from the "keys" blade in the Azure Portal. In Listing 5-1, you will see an example of our starter program. This example can be accessed at

https://learn.microsoft.com/en-us/azure/cosmos-db/sql/sql-api-get-started

Listing 5-1. .NET Getting Started

```
using System;
using System.Threading.Tasks;
using System.Configuration;
using System.Collections.Generic;
using System.Net;
using Microsoft.Azure.Cosmos;

public class Program
{
    // ADD THIS PART TO YOUR CODE

    // The Azure Cosmos DB endpoint for running this sample.
    private static readonly string EndpointUri = "<your endpoint here>";
    // The primary key for the Azure Cosmos account.
    private static readonly string PrimaryKey = "<your primary key>";

    // The Cosmos client instance
    private CosmosClient cosmosClient;

    // The database name.
    private Database database;

    // The container name.
    private Container container;

    // The name of the database and container we will create
    private string databaseId = "<YourDatabaseName";
    private string containerId = "<YourContainerName";
}
```

This starter code sets up some of the variables we will use in the next steps. To create a client, we need to create an instance of the *CosmosClient* class. We will do so in a method as shown in Listing 5-2.

Listing 5-2. Instantiate the CosmosClient

```
public async Task GetStartedDemoAsync()
{
    // Create a new instance of the Cosmos Client
    this.cosmosClient = new CosmosClient(EndpointUri, PrimaryKey);
}
```

While we are creating a connection, it is important to catch exceptions and handle them. We can achieve this by using a "try/catch" block and passing the *CosmosException* to be handled. See Listing 5-3 for an example.

Listing 5-3. Task Main with Try/Catch

```
public static async Task Main(string[] args)
{
    try
    {
        Console.WriteLine("Beginning operations...\n");
        Program p = new Program();
        await p.GetStartedDemoAsync();

    }
    catch (CosmosException cosmosException)
    {
        Console.WriteLine("Cosmos Exception with Status {0} : {1}\n",
        cosmosException.StatusCode, cosmosException);
    }
    catch (Exception e)
    {
        Console.WriteLine("Error: {0}", e);
    }
```

```
finally
{
    Console.WriteLine("End of demo, press any key to exit.");
    Console.ReadKey();
}
}
```

We can also access diagnostics from the data that is returned to our client. The *ItemResponse<T>* class that is returned by queries and point reads includes properties that are useful for diagnostics and troubleshooting. Two important properties of note are *RequestCharge*, which contains the RU cost for the request, and *Diagnostics*, which returns diagnostic information from the Azure Cosmos DB service.

I recommend you continue to follow the example from the link provided. There are additional methods that are provided to our client and that are relevant to the exam as well. *CreateDatabaseIfNotExistsAsync* is a method that will check for the existence of a database, and if none is found, it will be created for you. *CreateContainerIfNotExistsAsync* will perform the same check regarding containers. Both examples will provide developers with methods that allow for managing your Azure Cosmos DB instance using code. Once our database and container are created, how do we begin to add documents? The *CreateItemAsync* method will asynchronously add a new item to our container.

Querying items in our containers will be a common task in our clients. This can be achieved by using a standard SQL query (if using the SQL API) that is defined in a *QueryDefinition* object. The value of the query definition will be a string that contains our query like the example in Listing 5-4.

Listing 5-4. .NET SQL Query

```
private async Task QueryItemsAsync()
{
    var sqlQueryText = "SELECT * FROM c WHERE c.LastName = 'Andersen'";

    Console.WriteLine("Running query: {0}\n", sqlQueryText);

    QueryDefinition queryDefinition = new QueryDefinition(sqlQueryText);
    using FeedIterator<Family> queryResultSetIterator = this.container.Get
    ItemQueryIterator<Family>(queryDefinition);
```

```
List<Family> families = new List<Family>();

while (queryResultSetIterator.HasMoreResults)
{
    FeedResponse<Family> currentResultSet = await queryResult
    SetIterator.ReadNextAsync();
    foreach (Family family in currentResultSet)
    {
        families.Add(family);
        Console.WriteLine("\tRead {0}\n", family);
    }
}
}
```

But there is a more efficient way we can read items from an Azure Cosmos DB container called a *point read*. A point read requires the index of a single document. The index is the item's ID and partition key. If we submit *ReadItemAsync* while providing both the ID and the partition key, a point read will occur. Point reads are more efficient than queries as they remove the need to scan the entire physical partition and instead retrieve a specific document. In Listing 5-5, I have provided an example of a point read.

Listing 5-5. Point Read Operation in .NET

```
// Read existing item from container
Product readItem = await container.ReadItemAsync<Product>(
    id: "68719518388",
    partitionKey: new PartitionKey("gear-surf-surfboards")
);
```

We can also update items either by using the *ReplaceItemAsync* or *PatchItemAsync* methods. The PatchItemAsync method is easier to implement as we are only required to send the properties of the document that we wish to update. This prevents us from having to read and rebuild the entire object on the client side, improving latency and reducing development effort to interact with items in our container.

Azure Cosmos DB SDK Client Options

The Azure Cosmos DB SDK offers an object called *CosmosClientOptions* which allows you to set various options for the connectivity of your client. There are properties for bulk execution, preferred region, consistency level, connection mode, and request timeout, just to name a few. These options give instructions to the client and assist in accessing the functionality that you desire. Create, read, update, and delete (CRUD) and bulk write operations will be handled in a later chapter.

The connection mode of your client has an impact on the way the connection is established and maintained to your Azure Cosmos DB instance. There are two modes available: *gateway* mode and *direct* mode. Gateway mode is supported on all SDK platforms. Gateway mode is easier to implement as it uses standard HTTP ports and a single DNS endpoint to establish a connection to Azure Cosmos DB. When using gateway mode, your data plane requests will be routed to an intermediary gateway which then handles the request and routes it to the appropriate physical partitions. This extra hop introduces latency and overhead to your call but reduces the complexity.

Direct mode reduces latency by forgoing the need for the gateway intermediary. Instead, the client is sent metadata about the partition key ranges and the routing information required for queries to be delivered to the correct physical partition. The client will then open TCP connections to the physical partitions needed to serve the query without relying on the gateway. A downside of using direct mode is the range of ports that must be made available to the client to connect. When using gateway mode and the Core (SQL) API, only port 443 needs to be available. When switching to direct mode, 443 must be available as well as the range 10,000–20,000. This is a large range of ports and some organizations may receive pushback from security and compliance on opening these ports. If the client using direct mode is also leveraging private endpoints, all TCP ports should be open (0–65,535). The connection mode is defined in the CosmosClientOptions as stated earlier. You can see an example implementation in Listing 5-6.

Listing 5-6. Cosmos Client Option for Connectivity Mode

```
string connectionString = "<your-account-connection-string>";
CosmosClient client = new CosmosClient(connectionString,
new CosmosClientOptions
```

```
{
    ConnectionMode = ConnectionMode.Gateway // ConnectionMode.Direct is
    the default
});
```

Preferred region is an important option to understand for multi-region scenarios in Azure Cosmos DB. When multiple write regions are deployed in your account, how does the client know which instance to communicate with? The best region will be the region of closest proximity to the region your application is deployed to. For instance, if your application is deployed to East US 2, we do not want the application connecting to West US for its read operations due to the latency. We can tell our application which region it is deployed to by setting the *ApplicationRegion* property in our CosmosClientOptions.

Listing 5-7. Application Region in Cosmos Client Options

```
CosmosClient cosmosClient = new CosmosClient(
    "<connection-string-from-portal>",
    new CosmosClientOptions()
    {
        ApplicationRegion = Regions.WestUS2,
    });
```

By setting this property, the client will always connect to the region in closest proximity to its own. If additional regions are added to your Azure Cosmos DB account, no additional changes are required on the client. The client will always seek the lowest latency connection based on the ApplicationRegion property.

Azure Cosmos DB Emulator

When you are first exploring Azure Cosmos DB, you may not be ready to commit the budget to your project to support your account. In this case, there is a local emulator which allows you to become familiar with Azure Cosmos DB without creating a service in Azure. The Azure Cosmos DB Emulator is a locally installed program that emulates the cloud service. This allows you to develop and test your application locally without incurring any costs. To get started using the Emulator, download and install it using the following link:

```
https://aka.ms/cosmosdb-emulator
```

Using the Emulator, you can develop against the Core (SQL) API, the API for MongoDB, Cassandra, Gremlin, or Table.

The Emulator allows you to create, read, update, and delete data just as you would against the native cloud service. When you have completed your development and testing, it is easy to switch your connection information to your cloud hosted service on Azure. The parity between the Emulator and the native cloud service also includes authentication. The Emulator only supports connections via TLS just as the Azure service does. There is a default key provided in the documentation, but you can also generate your own key by providing the "/key" flag when starting the Emulator which will generate a new key for you on the fly.

Summary

Azure Cosmos DB is a robust, developer friendly platform. The SDKs provide functionality that allows the developer to control the way the client connects to the cloud instance of Azure Cosmos DB. This flexibility provides the high availability and global redundancy application developers require for critical applications. In this chapter, we explored an example application in the Microsoft Docs that will aid you in getting started in creating a client and connecting to an Azure Cosmos DB instance. The exam will expect you to understand the methods required to connect to, transact against, and manage your connections to your Azure Cosmos DB instance.

CHAPTER 6

Implement Data Access with Cosmos DB SQL

Accessing data from Azure Cosmos DB is very intuitive when using the NoSQL (SQL) API. SQL is a tried and true data access language that has been implemented in Azure Cosmos DB. But there are some important differences in accessing JSON documents versus a relational store. Queries can be issued from an IDE, an SDK, or from the Azure Cosmos DB Data Explorer. This chapter will explain the structure of queries and familiarize you with common operations such as SELECT, JOIN, and *sub-queries*. Understanding how to access your data will also help guide your data modeling decisions.

SQL Query Basics

To start with this topic, I recommend reading the following Microsoft Docs link. We will be referencing the same data model as we work through the queries.

```
https://learn.microsoft.com/en-us/azure/cosmos-db/nosql/query/
getting-started
```

Create the *Families* container and load the data per the link. Listing 6-1 shows what the data model looks like.

Listing 6-1. Families Data Model

```
{
  "id": "AndersenFamily",
  "lastName": "Andersen",
  "parents": [
    { "firstName": "Thomas" },
```

© Steve Flowers 2023

S. Flowers, *Designing and Implementing Cloud-native Applications Using Microsoft Azure Cosmos DB*, Certification Study Companion Series, https://doi.org/10.1007/978-1-4842-9547-2_6

```
        { "firstName": "Mary Kay"}
    ],
    "children": [
        {
            "firstName": "Henriette Thaulow",
            "gender": "female",
            "grade": 5,
            "pets": [{ "givenName": "Fluffy" }]
        }
    ],
    "address": { "state": "WA", "county": "King", "city": "Seattle" },
    "creationDate": 1431620472,
    "isRegistered": true
}
```

The unique ID for each document in this container will identify the family.
In Listing 6-1, you can see the document for the Andersen family. The Parents property
identifies two parents, and the Children property identifies the children of the parents. Both
properties are an array of sub-objects meaning that each element of the array is a JSON
document. The Address property is a *JSON literal* which is a single, nested JSON object.

Let's get started with the most basic SQL query of all: SELECT * FROM c which
returns all the items from the current container. When issuing queries from the SDK,
you will make a connection to a specific container as discussed in the last chapter. When
using the Azure Cosmos DB Data Explorer, highlight the container you wish to query
and click the "New SQL Query" button on the toolbar. The "c" from the inline example
earlier or the "f" from Listing 6-1 is a stand-in property representing the container we are
in. This is an arbitrary value not related to the container itself. This is in contrast to the
traditional SQL way, in which the table would be identified by the statement.

After retrieving all documents in our container, perhaps we want to retrieve a single
document. If we want to only return the Andersen family document, our query needs to
include a WHERE clause like in Listing 6-2.

Listing 6-2. Select Andersen Family Document

```
SELECT *
    FROM Families f
    WHERE f.id = "AndersenFamily"
```

After issuing this query, only the Andersen family document will be returned. In this case FROM Families f was included for clarity as to which container is being queried. Again, this is arbitrary and the container the query is issued against will return the results of the query. A limitation to be aware of in Azure Cosmos DB is that there are no cross-container queries.

Suppose we want to determine which family document was created first? We can leverage the built-in "_ts" property which represents the epoch time of the document. Listing 6-3 demonstrates this query, though it is not recommended to query by system properties as they could change in the future.

Listing 6-3. Select Document Order By

```
SELECT TOP 1 * FROM f
ORDER BY f._ts
```

The Andersen document is the only one returned because it was created first. This alludes to the fact that the ORDER BY clause sorts by ascending order by default. We can apply an explicit order by including the sort order in our clause like ORDER BY f._ts DESC, which will list the newest documents first which would have a higher "_ts" value.

Suppose we want to use a common *logical operator* like OR. In the case of our Families container, we may want to return documents that are only the Andersen family *or* the Wakefield family like in Listing 6-4.

Listing 6-4. Logical Operator OR

```
SELECT *
    FROM Families f
    WHERE f.id = "AndersenFamily" OR f.id = "WakefieldFamily"
```

In our first query, Listing 6-2, we used an equality operator when we included WHERE f.id = "AndersenFamily".

Several aggregates are also supported like Avg, Count, Max, Min, and Sum. The Count aggregate is an interesting example because it can be somewhat confusing. If you read the Microsoft Docs for "aggregate count," the syntax shows an argument of "any scalar expression." This is to say, like the container identifier, the argument is arbitrary and must only represent a scalar expression. As a refresher, a scalar expression is one that returns a single result. For instance, to count the number of documents in our Families container, we would issue the query SELECT Count(1) FROM f which will return

"$1" : 2. The "$1" represents an unnamed property that is returned from our query. We can simplify the output by placing the keyword VALUE in the statement like SELECT VALUE Count(1) FROM f, which removes the unnamed property and simply returns the value 2.

Advanced SQL Queries

The queries we looked at in the last section are fairly basic and operate very similarly to how SQL queries in the relational world behave. In this section, we will look at more advanced queries that interact with the complexities of a JSON document like nested objects, arrays, and sub-queries. Sub-queries are familiar territory for traditional SQL users but working with arrays and nested objects is likely unfamiliar to you unless you have worked with JSON data in classic SQL data stores.

First, we will look at the JOIN statement. In traditional SQL, this statement allows us to correlate data between different tables leveraging the normalized structure. In the NoSQL world, the JOIN statement is used to interact with properties of a document in a self-joining manner. Take, for example, a query which would retrieve all children of families in our Families container. We would use a JOIN statement to iterate over the "children" array and return the results that we are looking, as shown in Listing 6-5.

Listing 6-5. Basic Join on an Array

```
SELECT c.givenName
FROM Families f
JOIN c IN f.children
WHERE f.id = 'WakefieldFamily'
```

The results are projected from the lower level of the document (children) and surfaced to the top. We can interact with any of the properties that are within the array and even join to deeper levels. Look at the "pets" property of our document in Listing 6-1. We can create an additional join to surface the pet information to our query results as well as you can see in Listing 6-6.

Listing 6-6. Second-Level Join Correlation

```
SELECT
    f.id AS familyName,
    c.givenName AS childGivenName,
    c.firstName AS childFirstName,
    p.givenName AS petName
FROM Families f
JOIN c IN f.children
JOIN p IN c.pets
```

The results returned are presented in Listing 6-7.

Listing 6-7. Second-Level Join Results

```
[
    {

        "familyName": "AndersenFamily",
        "childFirstName": "Henriette Thaulow",
        "petName": "Fluffy"
    },
    {

        "familyName": "WakefieldFamily",
        "childGivenName": "Jesse",
        "petName": "Goofy"
    },
    {

        "familyName": "WakefieldFamily",
        "childGivenName": "Jesse",
        "petName": "Shadow"
    }
]
```

It is required to provide an alias to the properties since the query is considered a *multivalue tuple*. The tuple represents the results returned from our statements. When looking at the results, you can see a second document was created for "Jesse" as there is more than one pet name. We could not have two properties called "petName" on the same returned document, and the projection which iterates over the pet array creates a new document.

Type checking is an important aspect of data access to confirm the type of data that is being read. For instance, if a number is stored as a string, we can type check the property to determine how to handle it. In the case of a number stored as a string, we can introduce logic to type cast the string to an integer is our logic. Azure Cosmos DB includes several type checking functions to determine the types of properties on our documents:

- IS_ARRAY

- IS_BOOL

- IS_DEFINED

- IS_NULL

- IS_NUMBER

- IS_OBJECT

- IS_STRING

Type check functions can be used in your application logic to determine how to handle different structures. The function "IS_DEFINED" can help you determine if the property exists. This can be very helpful as the flexible nature of NoSQL means you may be reading a version of a document which has not implemented a specific property. The flexible schema of JSON means the properties may be added or removed as the use case of your application changes.

Finally, a common task when issuing queries to Azure Cosmos DB is the requirement to parametrize the queries. Parameters provide flexibility of user input as well as safeguards the query against SQL injection attacks. Parameterized queries can be implemented using the common "@" notation as displayed in Listing 6-8.

Listing 6-8. Parameterized Query

```
{
        "query": "SELECT * FROM Families f WHERE f.lastName = @lastName AND
        f.address.state = @addressState",
        "parameters": [
            {"name": "@lastName", "value": "Wakefield"},
```

```
        {"name": "@addressState", "value": "NY"},
    ]
}
```

Working with DateTimes

Azure Cosmos DB stores documents as JSON objects and JSON does not support a DateTime data type. DateTime properties must be stored as a string and the best practice for DateTime properties is to store them as UTC. As with any traditional data store, this reduces complexity in storing and understanding the time zone associated with the stored DateTime and can be converted on the fly as needed. Another benefit to storing DateTime as a UTC string is that range queries in Azure Cosmos DB are only supported if the UTC strings are of the same length and format. An alternative approach is to store the DateTime as epoch time, or Unix timestamp, that defines the number of seconds since January 1, 1970. Listing 6-9 represents an example document storing DateTime as UTC.

Listing 6-9. DateTime Stored as UTC in a String

```
{
        "id": "09152014101",
        "OrderDate": "2014-09-15T23:14:25.7251173Z",
        "ShipDate": "2014-09-30T23:14:25.7251173Z",
        "Total": 113.39
}
```

Though the DateTime is stored as a string, as long as we follow the *ISO 8601 format*, we have functions which can manipulate the DateTime property. The ISO 8601 standard describes a date format which is numeric and represents the number of milliseconds which have elapsed since the Unix epoch. The "OrderDate" in Listing 6-9 is an example of ISO 8601 format. Some functions that are useful and commonly used are *DateTimeAdd, DateTimeBin,* and *DateTimeDiff.*

The DateTimeAdd function provides the capability to add or remove units of time: years, months, days, hours, minutes, seconds, or milliseconds. We must supply a DateTime value as well as the DateTimePart (year, month, etc.) and an integer describing the value to increase or decrease. I have data loaded to an Azure Cosmos DB container which represents StackOverflow posts from 2013 to 2022. The posts include a

"_CreatedDate" property. Using the DateTime function DateTimeAdd, I can manipulate the results of the query. Suppose I want all posts created after June first of 2021. Listing 6-10 shows how I can use DateTimeAdd to add six months to the starting month of January meaning only posts created after June first will be returned.

Listing 6-10. DateTimeAdd Example

```
SELECT *
FROM c
WHERE c._CreationDate > DateTimeAdd('MM', 6, '2021-01-01 00:00:00.00')
```

DateTimeDiff is another useful function where we can compare two DateTime values to determine the difference in years, months, days, and so on. In our code we could parameterize two values to submit our query. Or, just to test this function we can add to static strings like Listing 6-11 where we determine that there is a two-year difference between 2021 and 2023.

Listing 6-11. DateTimeDiff Example

```
 SELECT DateTimeDiff('year', '2021-01-01 00:00:00.00', '2023-01-01
00:00:00.00') AS DifferenceInYears
```

A more advanced DateTime function is DateTimeBin. This function allows us to create "buckets" of time or groups of time based on the parameters selected and the input value. This can be very useful if you want to aggregate documents of these bins. In my example, I have the posts from StackOverflow container. Suppose I want to count total posts over weekly bins. Larger granularity time bins like year, month, and week are not supported. So instead we create bins on seven-day chunks. Listing 6-12 describes this query.

Listing 6-12. Example of DateTimeBin

```
SELECT DateTimeBin(c._CreationDate, 'd', 7) as week, Count(1) as TotalPosts
FROM c
GROUP BY DateTimeBin(c._CreationDate, 'd', 7)
```

The query created a bin on days with a bin size of seven which returns a count of all posts in a seven-day range. Listing 6-13 shows the output of this query.

Listing 6-13. Output of DateTimeBin

```
[
    {
        "week": "2022-10-06T00:00:00.0000000Z",
        "TotalPosts": 27086
    },
    {
        "week": "2022-09-29T00:00:00.0000000Z",
        "TotalPosts": 60534
    },
    {
        "week": "2022-09-22T00:00:00.0000000Z",
        "TotalPosts": 42835
    },
...
```

Summary

Querying data is made much easier by the implementation of a familiar SQL API in Azure Cosmos DB. In this section, we covered some of the basic operations you need to get started querying your data. The flexible nature of JSON documents allows our queries to dynamically access and project the properties in our documents in a way that fits our use case. The goal of this chapter was to additionally outline some of the aspects of querying JSON documents that are likely foreign to developers who have only written queries for relational systems. Beyond reading this chapter, I recommend following the chapter links provided and spending time working with different example data models to cement in your mind these important querying fundamentals.

## CHAPTER 7

Implement Data Access with SQL API SDKs

Again, we will spend some time discussing the various ways to access data and interact with Azure Cosmos DB using the SDK. By now, it should be obvious how important of a topic it is, considering the amount of content dedicated to it. The DP-420 test will expect you to know and understand how to interact with the Azure Cosmos DB service, databases, containers, and documents. In this chapter, we will dive deeper into the ways we can use the SDK to read, write, and update documents, load documents in bulk, and interact with document properties such as ETags and TTL.

Interacting with Documents

Interacting with discrete documents will be a common activity performed by your applications. Creating a new user profile, updating a product description, and deleting unneeded data are all common operators that you will implement in your application logic. Querying your documents, as covered in the last chapter, is also a common activity for retrieving your data and instantiating objects client side.

Creating new documents will be our first step and the examples I will share will leverage the newer v3 SDK. As you can see from Listing 7-1, creating a new document is accomplished by calling the *CreateItemAsync* method.

Listing 7-1. Create a New Document

```
ItemResponse<dynamic> response = await _container.
CreateItemAsync<dynamic>(item, new PartitionKey(partitionKeyValue));
```

© Steve Flowers 2023
S. Flowers, *Designing and Implementing Cloud-native Applications Using Microsoft Azure Cosmos DB*,
Certification Study Companion Series, https://doi.org/10.1007/978-1-4842-9547-2_7

CreateItemAsync, as it is aptly named, allows us to create a new JSON document asynchronously in our container. It is common to store the response of this object in an *ItemResponse* object which allows us to access properties on the response such as exceptions or the request charge of the operation.

Instead of a create operation, we can leverage the *Upsert* operation which will create a new document if none exists or update an existing document if it is found. The determination of the document's existence will rely upon the index of the document, as mentioned in previous chapters. The index of the document is the "id" field and the partition key. See Listing 7-2 for an example upsert.

Listing 7-2. Upsert a Document

```
Product createdItem = await container.UpsertItemAsync<Product>(
    item: newItem,
    partitionKey: new PartitionKey("gear-surf-surfboards")
);
```

Other than the upsert operation, Azure Cosmos DB supports a *Patch* operation. Patch is similar to upsert but includes additional granular functionality in interacting with properties. Patch also reduces development effort and network latency. Patch is easier to develop against because you only need to specify the value that you want to update, whereas in an upsert, you are rebuilding the entire object again in-memory. Patch allows you to specify the path to the property, the new value, and the type of operation. The operation types are add, set, replace, remove, and increment. The "add" operation is an upsert where it will add the property if it does not exist and update it if it does. It will also append to an array. Set is similar to add, except when working with arrays. If a valid index of an array is provided, that index will be updated. This contrasts to the append nature of the "add" operation type. Increment accepts both a positive and a negative integer which allows us to add or subtract from an integer value. Replace is also similar to add and set, but differs in that it will not create a new property, only update an existing property. If the property does not exist, an error will be thrown. To perform a patch operation, see Listing 7-3.

Listing 7-3. Document Patch Operation

```
ItemResponse<Product> response = await container.PatchItemAsync<Product>(
    id: "e379aea5-63f5-4623-9a9b-4cd9b33b91d5",
    partitionKey: new PartitionKey("road-bikes"),
    patchOperations: new[] {
        PatchOperation.Replace("/price", 355.45)
    }
);
```

As you can see in Listing 7-3, we are leveraging the method *PatchItemAsync*, and instead of specifying a JSON object, we are only providing the index of the document (id and partition key) as well as the operation. In this case, a "replace" operation is being performed on the "/price" property. The result will be the price property of the document and will be updated to "355.45." If the "/price" property does not exist, the patch will fail.

Deleting documents can be performed in two ways. The first is to execute the *DeleteItemAsync* method on a document while providing the ID and partition key as parameters. This works as you would expect and will be performed asynchronously. An alternative way to delete a document is to set the TTL (time to live) on a document. TTL can be set on the container level as covered in a previous chapter, but it can also be set at the item level. When set at the item level, the TTL value overwrites any TTL setting at the container level. This property is handy for documents that you don't want to be retained in your container for an extended period of time. This can be very useful for microservice applications which may be generating many events that are no longer relevant after a short period of time. TTL on the document is more efficient than explicitly deleting the document using the SDK. This is because the TTL of expired items is a background task that will only consume unused request units. This is beneficial for availability as the delete operation will not consume RUs that could be used by the application for create or update operations. However, by running as a background task, there is no guarantee when the operation will be performed. If the delete operation must be performed in a timely manner, use the SDK DeleteItemAsync method.

To set the TTL of a document, add the *DefaultTimeToLive* property to the document. Without this property, TTL will not be honored. If the TTL value is empty or null, the item will not be expired automatically unless by the container's TTL settings. Setting the TTL value to "-1" will ensure items do not expire. Any other nonzero value will ensure the document is expired *N* seconds after its last modified time.

Interacting with Many Documents

We've covered how to interact with a single document whether that be creating a new document or updating an existing document. However, you will often find yourself needing to transact against many documents. Whether that be loading a batch of new records into your container or retrieving a large batch of documents from your query. And sometimes, we will need those transactions to be *atomic* meaning that all should either succeed or all should fail.

Azure Cosmos DB supports multi-document transactional batch which provides atomicity. The operations of a transactional batch will either succeed together, or they will fail. As with traditional relational databases, a transaction is a sequence of operations that are logically grouped as a single unit of work. Each transaction comes with ACID guarantees, including atomicity. A limit to be mindful of regarding transactional batch is that it is limited to a single partition key. You will notice the partition key parameter is defined when creating a transactional batch. But let's take a look at creating a transactional batch in Listing 7-4.

Listing 7-4. Transactional Batch Operation

```
PartitionKey partitionKey = new PartitionKey("road-bikes");
TransactionalBatch batch = container.CreateTransactionalBatch(
partitionKey);

Product bike = new (
    id: "68719520766",
    category: "road-bikes",
    name: "Chropen Road Bike"
);

batch.CreateItem<Product>(bike);

Part part = new (
    id: "68719519885",
    category: "road-bikes",
    name: "Tronosuros Tire",
    productId: bike.id
);
```

```
batch.CreateItem<Part>(part);
```

```
using TransactionalBatchResponse response = await batch.ExecuteAsync();
```

As you can see in Listing 7-4, we must have a container object that identifies the container we plan to transact against as well as the partition key. In the example, "road-bikes" is the partition key that will be transacted against. We create a batch and store it in an object. Next, we add objects to the sequence of operations that will be executed in the batch. In the example, we are creating two new documents: a product document and a part document. Notice how they do not have the same schema; this is an example of the power of flexible schemas in NoSQL.

Creating batches has its benefits, but what about scenarios where there is a high number of documents that need to be created or updated? The SDK offers the *Bulk Executor* library which allows us to take advantage of the massive throughput of Azure Cosmos DB. The Bulk Executor library, which is supported for NoSQL (Core SQL API) and Gremlin APIs, significantly reduces the overhead of client communications to the server by creating a single-threaded connection to the service reducing the overhead of establishing sessions for multi-threaded operations. The Bulk Executor library also removes a lot of the tedium of managing application logic to interact with the Azure Cosmos DB service like rate limiting, error handling, timeouts, and so on. The Bulk Executor library will be diving documents based on the partition key and issue batches to the physical partitions where those partition key ranges reside. This process fully leverages the scale-out throughput of Azure Cosmos DB. In Listing 7-5, an example of leveraging the Bulk Executor library is shown for a bulk create (import) operation. The connection policy is set to "direct" and the protocol to "TCP." The client instantiates the Bulk Executor and issues the BulkImportAsync method passing a List of serialized JSON documents to be imported (documentsToImportInBatch).

Listing 7-5. Bulk Executor Example

```
ConnectionPolicy connectionPolicy = new ConnectionPolicy
{
    ConnectionMode = ConnectionMode.Direct,
    ConnectionProtocol = Protocol.Tcp
};
```

```
DocumentClient client = new DocumentClient(new Uri(endpointUrl),
authorizationKey,
```

```
connectionPolicy)

IBulkExecutor bulkExecutor = new BulkExecutor(client, dataCollection);

await bulkExecutor.InitializeAsync();

BulkImportResponse bulkImportResponse = await bulkExecutor.BulkImportAsync(
  documents: documentsToImportInBatch,
  enableUpsert: true,
  disableAutomaticIdGeneration: true,
  maxConcurrencyPerPartitionKeyRange: null,
  maxInMemorySortingBatchSize: null,
  cancellationToken: token);
```

Note   The Bulk Executor library is an implementation of the Azure Cosmos
DB SDK v2. Version 3 of the SDK simply implements this class for you and
only requires adding `CosmosClientOptions() { AllowBulkExecution`
`= true }`.

Transactional batch and the Bulk Executor library handle CRUD operations, but
what about scenarios where we want to read multiple documents from a query? Not all
queries are designed to return a discrete document and perhaps our aim is to return
multiple documents from our container such as all products in a customer's shopping
cart. Azure Cosmos DB has limitations in how much data can be returned in a single
page of a query. Each page of query results cannot exceed 4 MB of data. Additionally,
query execution time is capped at five seconds. Finally, some applications may only
want a limited number of items, for example, a search engine which would only want
to display the first 20 results on a page. In the SDK, we can iterate over multiple items
returned from a query. See Listing 7-6 for an example.

Listing 7-6. Query Multiple Documents

```
List<Family> familiesParallel1 = new List<Family>();
```

```
options.MaxConcurrency = 1;
using (FeedIterator<Family> query = container.GetItemQueryIterator<Family>(
    queryText,
    requestOptions: options))
  {
    while (query.HasMoreResults)
      {
        foreach (Family family in await query.ReadNextAsync())
        {
         familiesParallel1.Add(family);
        }
      }
  }
```

As you can see from Listing 7-6, we first create a list to store the results of the query. The "container.GetItemQueryIterator<Family>" call will continue to fetch items in the *while* loop as long as the query has more results. The results are added to the "familiesParallel1" list. This logic will exit once there are no more documents to fetch. Additionally, we can implement a continuation token to pick up where we left off if the process exits or is terminated. I will only show a few code snippets to display how to implement and use a continuation token, but a more complete example is included in this chapter's folder in the companion repository.

In Listing 7-7, we identify the setting of the continuation token contained in the response object. Next, we can use the continuation token in our FeedIterator to pick up where we left off. For instance, in the case of a search results page, we can set max item count to 10, store the continuation token, and later restart the query iterator with a new max item count and our continuation token. The query will then retrieve the next ten results from our query. The max item count in Listing 7-7 is set to "-1" which indicates that all documents should be retrieved. This will still honor the limits of query pages mentioned earlier in this section.

Listing 7-7. Query Iterator with Continuation Token

```
continuation = response.ContinuationToken;

// Resume query using continuation token
```

```
using (FeedIterator<Family> resultSetIterator = container.
GetItemQueryIterator<Family>(
        query,
        requestOptions: new QueryRequestOptions()
        {
            MaxItemCount = -1
        },
        continuationToken: continuation))
```

Session Control

Session control is important to understand as it offers flexibility in how we address our data in the Azure Cosmos DB service. In large-scale applications, where many clients are reading and updating data, we need mechanisms to ensure the data is in a consistent state before we act upon it. This prevents other clients from overwriting our work. For instance, if two clients are attempting to update an e-commerce shopping cart at the same time, without consistency controls some items in the shopping cart may be lost or overwritten. *Optimistic concurrency control* (OCC) allows you to avoid lost updates and deletes of your documents. If a client has read a document and plans to update it, how can we be sure that no other update was made on the document in the meantime? Also consider a situation where two clients are attempting to update the same document. How does the database know which version of the document is the most up to date to avoid losing intermediate updated?

These are common scenarios that are solved by OCC and rely on the "_etag" property of a document. Every document in an Azure Cosmos DB container will have an "_etag" property that is automatically generated on creation and updated whenever the document changes. This is all handled by the server anytime a document is created or updated. Our client can leverage the "_etag" property to ensure intermediate updates are not lost by implementing the "if-match" parameter in the request operation. The function of "if-match" is to check the current "_etag" stored in memory on the client with the value of the "_etag" for a document on the server. If they do not match, an exception is thrown. The client can use this exception to re-retrieve the document and reattempt the write operation. Look at Listing 7-8 for an example of implementation of optimistic concurrency control.

Listing 7-8. Optimistic Concurrency Control Check

```
//read item
ItemResponse<SalesOrder> itemResponse = await container.ReadItemAsync<Sales
Order>(partitionKey: new PartitionKey("Account1"),id: "SalesOrder1");

SalesOrder item = itemResponse;

updatedDoc = await container.ReplaceItemAsync<SalesOrder>(itemResponse,
item.Id, new PartitionKey(item.AccountNumber), new ItemRequestOptions {
IfMatchEtag = itemResponse.ETag });
```

As you can see, we retrieve a document and store the ItemResponse. Next, we attempt to update the document while also providing an *ItemRequestOptions* parameter and checking the "_etag" with *IfMatchEtag* of the previous stored ETag. If the Etag does not match, an exception will be thrown, and the client can reread the document before attempting to update again.

Azure Cosmos DB offers many flexible consistency options. Data consistency will be covered in depth in a later chapter, but for the benefit of session control, let's discuss the idea of *session consistency*. Session consistency ensures that clients can read their own writes consistently. When a write request is made to Azure Cosmos DB, the request is assigned a *SessionToken*. This token is used internally with each read and query to ensure that session consistency is maintained. Listing 7-9 shows an example of working with the session token on a subsequent read operation.

Listing 7-9. Capture and Read a Document with a Session Token

```
Container container = client.GetContainer(databaseName, collectionName);

ItemResponse<SalesOrder> response = await container.CreateItemAsync
<SalesOrder>(salesOrder);

string sessionToken = response.Headers.Session;

ItemRequestOptions options = new ItemRequestOptions();

options.SessionToken = sessionToken;

ItemResponse<SalesOrder> response = await container.ReadItemAsync<SalesOrder>
(salesOrder.Id, new PartitionKey(salesOrder.PartitionKey), options);
```

First, a SalesOrder item is created, and the response is stored. A new string variable "sessionToken" is created which stores the session token. The session token is then stored as an ItemRequestOptions object, and later, when ReadItemAsync is called, the options are passed as an argument.

Summary

In a scalable, high-throughput system like Azure Cosmos DB, it is important to have granular control over interactions with the database. When many clients are interacting with documents like in a microservice architecture, concurrency and latency become extremely important. The Azure Cosmos DB SDK provides controls to ensure clients maintain consistency and data is not lost or overwritten. The provided libraries for transactional batch and bulk execution both allow for consistent interaction and performant create and update operations. These tools are extremely valuable to developers leveraging Azure Cosmos DB and will be important for test takers in case studies and questions on the DP-420.

CHAPTER 8

Implement Server-Side Programming

Server-side programming in the way of *stored procedures, pre- and post-triggers*, and *user-defined functions* will be the focus of this chapter. Server-side programming allows you to package logic which is stored and precompiled for security, maintainability, and performance. Using JavaScript you can develop complex logic to be executed inside the database engine. Stored procedures also provide atomicity which can be useful for cases where all operations must succeed, or no operations can succeed. Packaging your logic server-side allows all clients to take advantage of the same logic, in the same way. This greatly reduces the burden on developers to maintain the logic on the client side. With server-side programming, you can query reference data on the fly for use in your operations, validate and alter properties as they are inserted, or quickly perform calculations. We'll start with how to create, deploy, and call stored procedures.

Implement Stored Procedures

Stored procedures can be created in the portal under a container in Azure Cosmos DB. If you expand the database and container where you want to create the stored procedure, you will see a drop-down for stored procedures as displayed in Figure 8-1.

© Steve Flowers 2023

S. Flowers, *Designing and Implementing Cloud-native Applications Using Microsoft Azure Cosmos DB*, Certification Study Companion Series, https://doi.org/10.1007/978-1-4842-9547-2_8

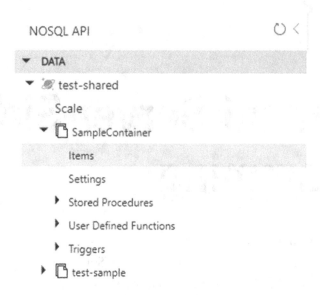

Figure 8-1. *List of Stored Procedures, UDFs, and Triggers*

To create a stored procedure, there is a button at the top of the Data Explorer window. Highlight the container where you would like to store the stored procedure and click the gears drop-down as pictured in Figure 8-2.

Figure 8-2. *Create New Stored Procedure*

Stored procedures can also be created using the SDK. This is referred to as "registering" the stored procedure. To provide logic for the stored procedure created using the SDK, a JavaScript file path is required. Once you've created a stored procedure, take a look at the sample provided. The sample is provided in Listing 8-1.

Listing 8-1. Sample Stored Procedure

```
// SAMPLE STORED PROCEDURE
function sample(prefix) {
```

```
var collection = getContext().getCollection();

// Query documents and take 1st item.
var isAccepted = collection.queryDocuments(
    collection.getSelfLink(),
    'SELECT * FROM root r',
function (err, feed, options) {
    if (err) throw err;

    // Check the feed and if empty, set the body to 'no docs found',
    // else take 1st element from feed
    if (!feed || !feed.length) {
        var response = getContext().getResponse();
        response.setBody('no docs found');
    }
    else {
        var response = getContext().getResponse();
        var body = { prefix: prefix, feed: feed[0] };
        response.setBody(JSON.stringify(body));
    }
});

if (!isAccepted) throw new Error('The query was not accepted by the
server.');
}
```

First, take note of the *getContext* method. The context object provides access to all the operations available in Azure Cosmos DB as well as access to request and response objects. In the sample, getContext is used to getCollection to retrieve a link to our collection. We can use this object to query items in the collection or create new items.

To call our stored procedure using the .NET SDK v3, we must call the *ExecuteStoredProcedureAsync* method. The required parameters are the stored procedure name, the partition key, and a list of items. As mentioned earlier, a stored procedure is performed against a single partition key. This is important to remember as it may drive your data model design. You may consider a partition key that will enable you to perform atomic transactions against a group of documents within a partition.

Listing 8-2 provides an example of calling a stored procedure from the SDK. Take special note of the ExecuteStoredProcedureAsync method, the return type (string), and the parameters.

Listing 8-2. Invoking a Stored Procedure

```
var result = await client.GetContainer("database", "container").
Scripts.ExecuteStoredProcedureAsync<string>("spCreateToDoItem", new
PartitionKey("Personal"), new[] { newItems });
```

Let's look at a more complex example of creating a document using a stored procedure. This example (Listing 8-3) is provided in the Microsoft documentation and a link to the document is included in the companion repository.

Listing 8-3. Stored Procedure to Create a New Item

```
function createToDoItems(items) {
    var collection = getContext().getCollection();
    var collectionLink = collection.getSelfLink();
    var count = 0;

    if (!items) throw new Error("The array is undefined or null.");

    var numItems = items.length;

    if (numItems == 0) {
        getContext().getResponse().setBody(0);
        return;
    }

    tryCreate(items[count], callback);

    function tryCreate(item, callback) {
        var options = { disableAutomaticIdGeneration: false };

        var isAccepted = collection.createDocument(collectionLink, item,
        options, callback);

        if (!isAccepted) getContext().getResponse().setBody(count);
    }
```

```
function callback(err, item, options) {
    if (err) throw err;
    count++;
    if (count >= numItems) {
        getContext().getResponse().setBody(count);
    } else {
        tryCreate(items[count], callback);
    }
}
}
```

Let's step through this code to understand what is happening. First, we get and store in a variable the collection and a link to the collection we want to act on. We set a *count* variable to "0" as we will loop through the data in the submitted list using a JavaScript *callback*. After checking for the existence of items and their length, we submit the first item to the *tryCreate* function. The tryCreate function enables the automatic generation of the "id" property. If this is set to "true," then we are telling Azure Cosmos DB that we don't have an "id" property and for the database engine to automatically generate a GUID.

Next, we submit the *createDocument* operation and store the results in a variable. You will see that the *callback* is issued on this method which basically creates a loop. The callback increases the *count* variable and determines if there are items left to create. If there are more items, the *tryCreate* function is called again. This loop will continue until all the items have been submitted for creation.

I highly recommend not only spending time with the documentation to cement your understanding of the stored procedure functionality, but also spending time implementing and calling these stored procedures in the SDK. This will ensure that the concepts and methods are embedded in your memory and ready to be recalled for the DP-420 exam.

Triggers and User-Defined Functions

Triggers and user-defined functions allow us additional flexibility by leveraging server-side programming. There are two types of triggers: pre-triggers and post-triggers. Pre-triggers are executed ***before*** creating or updating a database item and post-triggers are executed ***after*** creating or updating a database item. Triggers are not executed automatically, however. They must be called with each individual database operation where you want them to operate. Pre-triggers and post-triggers cannot have any input parameters and instead use the item or document that is defined in the operation.

As an example, take a "create" operation where we want to ensure that a timestamp property is present on the document. Pre-triggers and post-triggers require a definition of the types of operations that can run it. The supported operations are All, Insert, Replace, and Delete. To ensure the timestamp is present, we would define and register our pre-trigger and execute the pre-trigger in our requestOptions in our Azure Cosmos DB client in the SDK. The pre-trigger will then add the timestamp property to the document before insert, if the property is missing. See Listings 8-4 and 8-5 from the Microsoft documentation for an example.

Listing 8-4. Define a Pre-trigger for Timestamp Property

```
function validateToDoItemTimestamp() {
    var context = getContext();
    var request = context.getRequest();

    // item to be created in the current operation
    var itemToCreate = request.getBody();

    // validate properties
    if (!("timestamp" in itemToCreate)) {
        var ts = new Date();
        itemToCreate["timestamp"] = ts.getTime();
    }

    // update the item that will be created
    request.setBody(itemToCreate);
}
```

Listing 8-5. Execute a Pre-trigger in the SDK

```
dynamic newItem = new
{
    category = "Personal",
    name = "Groceries",
    description = "Pick up strawberries",
```

```
    isComplete = false
};

Uri containerUri = UriFactory.CreateDocumentCollectionUri("myDatabase",
"myContainer");
RequestOptions requestOptions = new RequestOptions { PreTriggerInclude =
new List<string> { "trgPreValidateToDoItemTimestamp" } };
await client.CreateDocumentAsync(containerUri, newItem, requestOptions);
```

In Listing 8-4, we will see that if the timestamp property does not exist (!), we get the current datetime and apply it to the property before writing the document. In listing 8-5, the pre-trigger is called by defining the trigger in our requestOptions and passing those options as a parameter to our CreateDocumentAsync call. Post-triggers operate in the same way as pre-triggers except for the fact post-triggers run as part of the same transaction. With post-triggers, if the execution fails, the entire transaction will fail.

User-defined functions (UDFs) are packaged logic that allows us to extend the SQL syntax with custom application logic. UDFs allow you to define business logic within your server-side code such as mathematical operations, transformations on a property, and filtering. UDFs should be avoided if a system function already exists that performs the logic you are trying to achieve. You should also avoid UDFs where the UDF would be the only filter in a WHERE clause as UDFs to not leverage the index and loading documents will be more expensive. Listing 8-6 shows an example UDF from the Microsoft documentation. The goal of this UDF is to calculate the tax burden for an employee by accepting their income as an input parameter. A UDF will return a single scalar value for each document evaluated, so keep that in mind when determining the appropriate use case for UDFs.

Listing 8-6. UDF to Calculate Tax Based on Income

```
function tax(income) {
    if (income == undefined)
        throw 'no input';

    if (income < 1000)
        return income * 0.1;
    else if (income < 10000)
        return income * 0.2;
```

```
    else
        return income * 0.4;
}
```

Summary

Server-side programming via stored procedures, triggers, and user-defined functions provides extensibility and maintainability in your logic when programming against Azure Cosmos DB. Stored procedures allow atomicity while increasing performance and maintainability by packaging your business logic and executing that logic on the database engine. Triggers allow you to validate and transform the properties of your documents while removing the logic from your client-side code. UDFs can expand your queries to include new projections and filters defined by your internal business logic. Together, these tools provide a very flexible development experience for developers that can unlock performance, maintainability, and efficiency.

CHAPTER 9

Design and Implement a Replication Strategy

Azure Cosmos DB is a scalable, globally distributed NoSQL database engine. With a single click, new instances of the service can be created in regions all over the world. Adding additional regions provides your application with the ability to bring your data closer to your users, greatly reducing latency. Unlike most technologies that allow you to create read replicas or cache data in memory to reduce read latency, Azure Cosmos DB allows you to create write replicas near your users. Azure Cosmos DB offers both *multi-region* deployments where there is a single write region and $N + 1$ read regions or *multi-write* deployments which offers $N + 1$ write regions. The availability of multi-write functionality brings many benefits to globally dispersed workloads, but it also brings some challenges. Azure Cosmos DB automatically synchronizes the data between regions for you. But if data is being written from multiple locations, how can we maintain *data consistency*?

Data consistency is the perspective that all instances of your application have of your data. If someone on the West coast of the United States is reading a document which is also being written to by someone in the European Union, how does Azure Cosmos DB provide consistency? Azure Cosmos DB provides five different levels of consistency to find the right fit for your application. In this chapter we will dive into the global replication abilities of Azure Cosmos DB and discuss how to determine the best consistency level of your data.

© Steve Flowers 2023
S. Flowers, *Designing and Implementing Cloud-native Applications Using Microsoft Azure Cosmos DB*, Certification Study Companion Series, https://doi.org/10.1007/978-1-4842-9547-2_9

Global Distribution

Global distribution of data serves two purposes in our Azure Cosmos DB environments. The first, mentioned in the introduction to this chapter, is to bring an instance of your database engine closer to your users. This greatly reduces latency and improves the user experience for your application. Compare this to a monolithic application where there is a primary database thousands of miles away from its end users. When your data engine is thousands of miles away, users experience long load times, spinning wheel loading screens, and general high latency interaction with your application.

Even when most of your users are in one global region, additional regions bring reliability to your application. Multiple regions in Azure Cosmos DB increase the high availability and disaster recovery of your application. By adding a secondary read region, you can ensure that during an outage clients are seamlessly redirected to the secondary region after a failover. For critical applications which are globally dispersed, multiple write regions will ensure that clients can continue to work with your application through the loss of a single region, or multiple regions. It is recommended that accounts are configured with at least a second read region for high availability and disaster recovery.

Adding additional regions to your Azure Cosmos DB is easy. See Figure 9-1. In the Azure Portal, navigate to your Azure Cosmos DB account. The box marked "1" displays the "Replicate data globally" blade which allows access to add and remove regions as well as perform failover. Box "2" displays the toggle to make your account multi-region (one write region, one or many read regions) or multi-write (one or more write regions). Box "3" displays the option to add additional regions.

When you add a new region, a drop-down will allow you to select the location of that region. If availability zones are available for that region, it must be selected at time of creation. Finally, box "4" displays a map view of all the available regions. In the map view, hexagons with the "+" symbol are regions where new instances can be created. Hexagons with the check symbol are regions where you have already provisioned an instance of your account. As you add regions, you will see them added to your list of regions to the right of the screen. The order of the regions is significant as it determines the failover priority. If your primary region fails, the next region in the list will be elected the primary. Just remember, adding regions is a multiplier on your provisioned throughput, and as such, a multiplier on your cost.

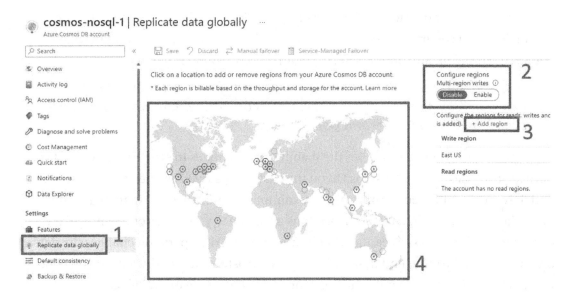

Figure 9-1. *Replicate Data Globally*

Azure Cosmos DB supports two failover methods: *service-managed* failover and *manual* failover. Enabling service-managed failover ensures that in the case of a regional outage, a new region is elected as the primary. Failures are detected and failover initiated automatically. In the case of a failover, there are no changes required on the client. Manual failover allows the admin of the Azure Cosmos DB account to initiate a failover for the account. This may be required due to telemetry in logs, other services in the architecture needing to failover, or to perform maintenance on a specific region (primarily, adding a new availability zone enabled region). An important note on manual failover: it is a graceful failover. If the data is not in a consistent state, a manual failover will fail. It is best to rely on service-enabled failover. In the case of a multi-write configuration, service-managed failover is not supported and not applicable due to the nature of having multiple write instances. In the case of a failure, a region will be marked offline, and clients will read the next closest instance to their geographic location.

Data Consistency

In a distributed data system such as Azure Cosmos DB, data must be replicated between instances of the engine. This introduces some problems regarding data consistency. The problems present themselves in the form of trade-offs. Before we dive further into consistency, let's discuss a key theorem that frames the issue for us. The *PACELC* theorem defines the physical limitations of data which is replicated between locations and maintains a congruent view for users of that data. PACELC is an acronym which defines the problem and outlines the trade-offs. The theorem is defined as

> In the case of network **P**artitioning, you must choose between **A**vailability and **C**onsistency. **E**lse, when everything is operating nominally, you must choose between **L**atency and **C**onsistency.

Network partitioning describes the inability of two nodes to synchronize data. If you have an instance of Azure Cosmos DB on the east coast as well as one on the west coast, and they are unable to communicate, they cannot synchronize data. In this case you must choose between making both locations available to your users or ensuring data consistency. If the two sites cannot synchronize and a write operation changes the data on one end, on the other end there will be an inconsistent view of the data. If you choose to remain consistent, then one of the instances must be made unavailable.

When everything is operating nominally, we must still consider the physical requirements for moving data. If we have an instance in the Central US and another in Germany, there is a real-time cost to synchronize that data. The latency of synchronizing data between the two sites is likely 100ms or more. While data is being synchronized, clients may have an inconsistent view of the data. So we must choose between latency, or how quickly we want a client to conclude their operation, and consistency, or how congruent the view of data is for different clients. The lower the latency, the greater the risk of inconsistency. The more consistency, the higher the latency.

Azure Cosmos DB offers five different consistency modes providing extreme flexibility for your use case. These variable options allow you to fine-tune the trade-offs found in distributed data systems. These consistency modes are

- Strong

- Bounded staleness

- Session

- Consistent prefix

- Eventual

Strong consistency provides the highest level of consistency for read operations. A client will always see the most recent, committed version of a document. Strong consistency has the highest level of consistency but comes with increased latency. A client writing a document must wait for the document to be replicated before their operation is successful. This equates to lower latency for the client as this is a synchronous operation. As we move down the list, we will trade off consistency for lower latency. Consider using strong consistency when data consistency is important above all else. A banking application, for instance, would rather have the user experience higher latency than present two different values on an account or a cryptocurrency trading application which services buy and sell orders which would be accountable if a user was presented with a different currency price as compared to a user in another region.

Bounded staleness provides a time interval which defines how far reads can lag behind writes. This interval is defined as "K" (the number of versions of a document) and "T" (the amount of time). For a single region account, the minimum of K and T is 10 write operations or 5 seconds. This means that reads will lag behind write at most by 10 write operations or 5 seconds, whichever comes first. Consider bounded staleness for applications which can trade some consistency for a lower latency. Bounded staleness preserves global ordering which means even when consistency has decreased, eventually a user will realize writes in the order that they were issued. Bounded staleness is often chosen for collaboration applications, where low latency means a better user experience but the data consistency does not equate to risk. Also consider streaming applications, *pub/sub*, and telemetry. The lag interval provides great flexibility in defining the trade-off between consistency and latency.

Session consistency is aligned to a client session and their perspective on the data. Session consistency provides a "Read Your Writes" guarantee which means a client within a session will have a consistent view of the data, but clients outside of the session may see stale data. Consider applications which are primarily focused around the user experience: online shopping product recommendation engines, music streaming profiles and playlists, or "to-do" list type applications. These kinds of applications are primarily focused on the activities of one or a few users. Multiple users with the need to share the same perspective and consistency of the data can share a session. But clients outside of that session will have a consistent prefix consistency on the same data.

Consistent prefix consistency continues to lower the strength of the consistency, but continues to lower the latency. There is no controlling the timeframe in which writes are replicated, but consistent prefix guarantees that the writes will be in order. Similarly to consistent prefix, eventual consistency makes no guarantee on when the data will be replicated. Unlike consistent prefix, eventual consistency also makes no guarantee as to the order of the updates. Consider using consistent prefix when you want low latency, eventual consistency is fine, but you want to ensure that the order of operations is retained. Both consistency modes would be suitable for applications with the strictest requirements for low latency. Consider a microservices application that asynchronously reads and updates documents. Microservices often need to transact quickly and move on. If that same application also cares about the ordering of operations, consistent prefix would be the right choice. A social media application may not care about the order of operations. As a user interacts with their phone to post an update or a photo, they simply want the process to happen as quickly as possible. Can you imagine the user's reaction if it took ten seconds to post a comment on a friend's post? Eventual consistency guarantees that the client leveraged by the social media application can submit the post and return a successful response to the application so the user can move on. The data will be replicated eventually. At worse in this scenario, a distant relative will see your post a few seconds after you actually posted it.

One last consideration for your consistency selection is cost. Reads and writes against a consistency level have a quorum requirement which dictates how many nodes in the local region as well as how many nodes in remote regions must participate in the operation. The more nodes that are required to participate in the operation, the more costly the operation in terms of RU and ultimately billing. Table 9-1 describes the quorum requirements for each consistency model. As you can see, writes operating against a strong consistency will come with the highest cost as a quorum among a majority of nodes in a majority of regions must be reached. If there are three regions in your account, two out of the three will need to acknowledge the operation.

Table 9-1. *Consistency Level Quorum*

Consistency Level	Quorum Reads	Quorum Writes
Strong	Local Minority	Global Majority
Bounded Staleness	Local Minority	Local Majority
Session	Single Replica (using session token)	Local Majority
Consistent Prefix	Single Replica	Local Majority
Eventual	Single Replica	Local Majority

Global Distribution Configurations in the SDK

At the account level, we control which regions our Azure Cosmos DB instance is deployed to and can control the priority of those regions when it comes to failover. As mentioned earlier, the priority is defined by the list of regions in a top-down order. If the first region in the list fails, the next in the list will be elected as the write region. However, clients can control which regions they connect to. This provides the benefit of clients connecting to the region which will bring the lowest latency based on their geographic location. There are two ways to define the priority of regions in the SDK. One is to define the *preferred regions*, and another is to define the client's *application region*.

The preferred regions configuration is available as a Cosmos client option. The "ApplicationPreferredRegions" property accepts a list of region names. See Listing 9-1 from the Microsoft documentation.

Listing 9-1. Application Preferred Regions

```
CosmosClientOptions options = new CosmosClientOptions();
options.ApplicationName = "MyApp";
options.ApplicationPreferredRegions = new List<string> {Regions.WestUS,
Regions.WestUS2};

CosmosClient client = new CosmosClient(connectionString, options);
```

From the example you can see that both the West US and West US2 regions were added to a list and set as the property for "ApplicationPreferredRegions". If West US becomes unavailable, the client will opt to use West US2. If either region is unavailable, the client will use the current primary write region.

Instead of explicitly defining the regions on behalf of the client, we can set the application region in Cosmos client options. By setting the client's region, the SDK will decide which region is closest to the client and choose the best region. This value should be set for the geographically dispersed instances of your application to allow Azure Cosmos DB to handle the work of selecting the appropriate region. See Listing 9-2 from the Microsoft documentation for an example.

Listing 9-2. Application Region in the SDK

```
CosmosClientOptions options = new CosmosClientOptions();
options.ApplicationName = "MyApp";
// If the application is running in West US
options.ApplicationRegion = Regions.WestUS;

CosmosClient client = new CosmosClient(connectionString, options);
```

In addition to having control over which regions the client reads from and writes to, the client can override the default consistency level set on the account. It is important to note that the consistency level *can only be relaxed* in the client. This means if the default consistency of the Azure Cosmos DB account is "strong," the client can relax the consistency to bounded staleness. If the default consistency is "consistent prefix," the client can only relax the consistency to "eventual." The "relaxing" refers to the level of consistency. As mentioned earlier, the list is ordered starting with strong and moving to eventual by the level of consistency. This can be accomplished in the SDK by setting the "ItemRequestOptions" consistency level to a more relaxed level. See an example in Listing 9-3 from the Microsoft documentation.

Listing 9-3. Relaxing the Default Consistency Level

```
// Override consistency at the request level via request options
ItemRequestOptions requestOptions = new ItemRequestOptions {
ConsistencyLevel = ConsistencyLevel.Strong };

var response = await client.GetContainer(databaseName, containerName)
    .CreateItemAsync(
        item,
        new PartitionKey(itemPartitionKey),
        requestOptions);
```

Summary

Distributed data comes with a lot of considerations and these considerations come with trade-offs. It is important to understand your workload to prepare for the right configuration that fits your use case. It is also important to be comfortable in making changes to these configurations later to suit your application if your initial configuration is not optimal. Azure Cosmos DB provides amazing flexibility to meet the needs of your global distributed application by making it easy to create and distribute data to new regions around the world and offering five different levels of consistency. This flexibility is extended to the SDK for developers to choose the appropriate read/write regions and set the consistency needs for their specific use cases.

Summary

## CHAPTER 10

Design and Implement Multi-region Write

Multi-region writes in Azure Cosmos DB brings low-latency write operations to your global workloads where client write latency and availability is of the utmost importance. The ability to create additional write regions provides an instance of your database closer to your users but introduces some new challenges. Write conflicts can occur in a multi-region scenario since users in two different regions could be attempting to write the same document. Multi-write also comes with increased availability for writes. When your account has multiple write regions, if one of the regions becomes unavailable the SDK will automatically write to another available region. Compared to a single write region configuration which would require a service managed failover for write availability, a multi-write configuration provides fast, seamless write availability. In this chapter we will review how to work with multi-region configurations in the SDK as well as how to resolve conflicts that arise in Azure Cosmos DB.

When to Use Multi-region Write

Multi-region writes bring a lot of flexibility to your Azure Cosmos DB design. However, it is not appropriate for all use cases. Consider multi-region writes when write availability is very important for your application. For example, a social media application would rather accept a new post from a user than return a failure to the user. This could damage the reputation of an application as it degrades the user experience. Keep in mind this differs from read availability. Another use case for multi-write regions is latency of writes. In the case of IoT applications like connected vehicles or smart meters, having Azure Cosmos DB instances globally dispersed and accepting write operations will greatly reduce your latency.

93

© Steve Flowers 2023
S. Flowers, *Designing and Implementing Cloud-native Applications Using Microsoft Azure Cosmos DB*, Certification Study Companion Series, https://doi.org/10.1007/978-1-4842-9547-2_10

Read availability is concerned more with the consistency of the data being provided. As mentioned in the introduction to this chapter, multi-region writes cannot support strong consistency. Multi-write brings latency benefits to your application but does not provide the highest level of read availability. To achieve the highest level of read availability, a single-region write configuration should be used with strong consistency.

Consider an IoT scenario where meters all over the world are emitting temperature measurements that you want to store in Azure Cosmos DB. In a real-time analytics scenario, the goal is to ingest these messages as quickly as possible. IoT devices typically produce a large volume of data and ingesting this data as quickly as possible will allow the business to make real-time decisions. Multi-write in this scenario will ensure that the latency for meters which are geographically dispersed are able to write to Azure Cosmos DB quickly. The low latency provided by the multi-write configuration will ensure that data is ingested quickly and the client performing the write operation can move on to new messages. From an availability perspective, we would rather the clients are seamlessly redirected to another write region during an outage. Though some consistency could be lost while the primary write region for a client is down, the ability to continue to ship telemetry that downstream processes require for business function may justify this trade-off.

Implement Multi-region Write

Configuring your Azure Cosmos DB account for multi-write is simple. In Figure 10-1, see box 2. This toggle will enable or disable multi-region writes for your account.

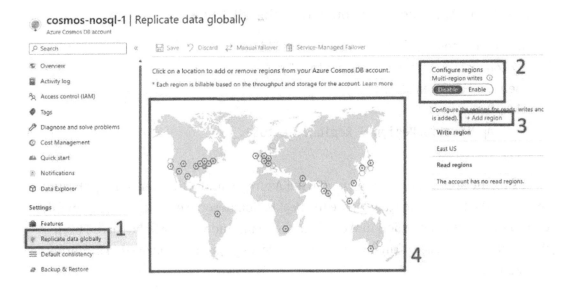

Figure 10-1. *Configure Multi-region Writes*

Multi-region writes can also be enabled using PowerShell. See Listing 10-1 for an example.

Listing 10-1. Enable Multi-region Writes in PowerShell

```
Update-AzCosmosDBAccount `
    -ResourceGroupName $resourceGroupName `
    -Name $accountName `
    -EnableMultipleWriteLocations:$enableMultiMaster
```

Azure CLI is also supported. See Listing 10-2.

Listing 10-2. Enable Multi-region Writes in Azure CLI

```
az cosmosdb update --ids $accountId --enable-multiple-write-locations true
```

In this book we have covered the .NET SDK v3. However, I do want to point out a quality-of-life update that was made in v3 versus v2. In version 2 of the SDK, it was required to set the property "UseMultipleWriteLocations" to "true" in your connection policy. In version 3 however, it is as simple as setting the "ApplicationRegion" property as discussed in the last chapter. Take a look at Listing 10-3 as a reminder of how to implement the client application region.

Listing 10-3. Application Region in v3 of the .NET SDK

```
CosmosClient cosmosClient = new CosmosClient(
    "<connection-string-from-portal>",
    new CosmosClientOptions()
    {
        ApplicationRegion = Regions.WestUS2,
    });
```

Using the application region, we can tell Azure Cosmos DB where our application resides and let the service determine the best region to serve operations from. In this case, if there is a write region in West US 2, the reads and writes will be served from that region. In the case of an outage, the next closest region will be used to perform operations.

Conflict Resolution

Conflict resolution is an important concept in a multi-region write scenario. If a client in West US and another client in East US are attempting to update the same document, a conflict can occur. Azure Cosmos DB has a *PATCH* API which can update specific attributes of a document. This patch API allows us to avoid conflicts against documents where users are updating different attributes. But if two users are attempting to update the same attributes on the same document, a conflict will arise.

How do we resolve this conflict? Which update should be retained when everything is said and done? These questions offer an insight into why strong consistency is not available in a multi-region write configuration. As a reminder, strong consistency will attempt to replicate a write operation before returning a success message to the client. If two clients in two different regions attempt to update the same document, there is no way for strong consistency to be honored as both operations would conflict and there would be no way to recover. The source of this behavior is the non-locking characteristic of Azure Cosmos DB.

There are two conflict resolution policies that are supported in Azure Cosmos DB. The most basic is *last write wins* (LWW) which defines the winner of the conflict as the write operation with the highest "_ts" attribute. Another property can be defined for LWW as long as it is a numeric type. This could apply to a self-incrementing ID or another customer attribute. Listing 10-4 shows an example from the Microsoft documentation on implementing the LWW policy. This must be performed from the SDK and can only be configured for new containers.

Listing 10-4. Last Write Wins Policy on a Container

```
Container container = await createClient.GetDatabase(this.databaseName)
    .CreateContainerIfNotExistsAsync(new ContainerProperties(this.lww
    CollectionName, "/partitionKey")
    {
        ConflictResolutionPolicy = new ConflictResolutionPolicy()
        {
            Mode = ConflictResolutionMode.LastWriterWins,
            ResolutionPath = "/myCustomId",
        }
    });
```

This conflict resolution policy is very straightforward and requires little thought, which makes it simple. However, it is also quite limiting. You may not have an obvious attribute to use for LWW or the "_ts" property may not be the best definition for the logic of your application regarding resolving a conflict. In this case, a custom conflict resolution policy can be created.

A custom conflict resolution policy allows us to define a stored procedure in Azure Cosmos DB to determine what to do with conflicting documents. The stored procedure follows the same configuration and rules of standard stored procedures in that they are written in Javascript and must operate against a single partition. When we define a custom conflict resolution policy for a container, we provide the stored procedure that will be called to resolve conflicts. There are parameters that must be implemented in order for a stored procedure to work as a custom conflict resolution policy. These are as follows:

- *incomingItem*: The item being inserted that is involved in the conflict

- *existingItem*: The item that has already been committed that is involved in the conflict

- *isTombstone*: A boolean value indicating if the incomingItem is in conflict with a previously deleted item

- *conflictingItems*: An array of existingItems that conflict with the incomingItem on the conflict property defined

The stored procedure can interact with any documents within a single partition. If an incoming item is in conflict with a single document or multiple documents, these parameters can be used to compare attributes to determine how to resolve the conflict. As an example, consider a logistics company where two different warehouses are requesting a truck to route to their location for a pickup. LWW may not be the best approach in this situation as the organization may want to take other factors into consideration when making the decision. For instance, we could evaluate the truck's current location and choose the request which is geographically closer to reduce the amount of extra travel the truck would have to make. Instead of simply using LWW, we would evaluate the last item committed for the truck to determine its current location, and compare the two conflicting document's location property, and commit the one that is the closest.

To create a custom conflict resolution policy, first we must create the stored procedure that will be used to resolve the conflicts. Once the stored procedure is in place, it can be defined as the "ResolutionProcedure" on the "ConflictResolutionPolicy" for our container. Listing 10-5 has an example of creating a new container implementing a custom conflict resolution policy on a container.

Listing 10-5. Custom Conflict Resolution Policy on a Container

```
Container container = await createClient.GetDatabase(this.databaseName)
    .CreateContainerIfNotExistsAsync(new ContainerProperties(this.
    udpCollectionName, "/partitionKey")
    {
        ConflictResolutionPolicy = new ConflictResolutionPolicy()
        {
            Mode = ConflictResolutionMode.Custom,
            ResolutionProcedure = string.Format("dbs/{0}/colls/{1}/sprocs/
            {2}", this.databaseName, this.udpCollectionName, "resolver")
        }
    });
```

In this case, our stored procedure is named "resolver", however, the stored procedure can be named anything. This resolution procedure will be enacted whenever there is a conflict. For an example stored procedure, see the link provided in the companion repository for "Configure conflict resolution policies."

Summary

Multi-region writes provide low latency and high availability for write-critical workloads. The ability to provide additional write regions provides flexibility in your application but will introduce new challenges to contend with. For any multi-region write scenario, it is important to understand how to implement multi-write as well as resolve conflicts. Last write wins resolution is a simple and fast way to resolve conflicts but custom conflict resolution policies handled by a stored procedure provide the flexibility to define a resolution policy that makes sense for your application.

## CHAPTER 11

Enable Analytical Workloads

Azure Cosmos DB is a *hybrid transactional and analytical platform* (HTAP), which means its APIs serve both transactional workloads and analytical workloads at the same time. This functionality is provided by the *analytical store* in Azure Cosmos DB. In most architectures, ETL is required to extract data from your transactional store and load it into an intermediary store for transformation and serving to BI workloads. By leveraging the analytical store in Azure Cosmos DB, we can access data in our account without consuming request units and access the data in a columnar format. These are two key benefits Azure Cosmos DB analytical store provides compared to other platforms. In this chapter, I will demonstrate how you can use features of Azure Cosmos DB to serve your analytical workloads. This is an important part of managing an operational system to enable business intelligence while not affecting your application's performance.

Hybrid Transaction and Analytical Platform

ETL (or ELT) is the process of extracting data from your transactional data stores for analytics. Typically, this involves an ETL tool which can connect to the data store to extract the data, perform transformations, and land the data somewhere analysts can access for reporting. The most common pattern today is ELT, where the data is extracted, landed in a data stored, then transformed. If we consider a basic architecture of an application that uses Azure SQL for its data store, the process for performing analytics of that data may look like this:

1. Implement Azure Data Factory and connect to Azure SQL.

© Steve Flowers 2023
S. Flowers, *Designing and Implementing Cloud-native Applications Using Microsoft Azure Cosmos DB*,
Certification Study Companion Series, https://doi.org/10.1007/978-1-4842-9547-2_11

2. Define a data landing zone, commonly Azure Storage as a data lake.

3. Create a pipeline to copy data from Azure SQL to Azure Storage.

4. Validate the data and perform transformations.

5. Land the transformed data in a curated layer of the Azure Storage account.

6. Serve the data from Synapse Analytics or Power BI Premium.

When leveraging the analytical store, the Azure Cosmos DB service automatically converts your row store data (JSON documents) to a columnar format. It does this without consuming RUs and thus does not impact your transactional workload. This is a zero ETL approach to access the data in your Azure Cosmos DB account. Data is automatically synchronized to the analytical store within two minutes. In cases your database is leveraging shared throughput with many containers, the sync could take up to five minutes.

Once data is available in the analytical store, you can connect to and work with that data from Azure Synapse leveraging Azure Synapse Link. Using either the serverless SQL pool or Spark, you can query, transform, and copy your data. In the process outlined earlier, Azure Data Factory connecting to Azure Cosmos DB would consume RUs making the process costly and would impact your transactional workload. With the analytical store, we can access the data at a lower cost and much more easily when using Azure Synapse Link.

The database engine automatically converts your row store to a columnar store and this brings many benefits for analytical workloads. Columnar data can be compressed up to 90% and the cost of storing that data is greatly reduced. The analytical store data is stored in Azure Storage. The low cost of Azure Storage coupled with the compression that comes from using a columnar store greatly reduces cost. With the automatic conversion from a row store to a columnar store, naturally the question arises on how a flexible schema can be converted to a structured schema in a columnar store. The analytical store implements automatic schema inference which allows schema changes in the transactional store to automatically be included in the analytical store.

But how does all of this work with the geographically distributed nature of Azure Cosmos DB? When your account is in a multi-region configuration, there is an analytical store in each region. If your account has regions in both East US and Europe, both regions will be able to access the analytical store in their perspective region.

This is very beneficial for organizations which may have analytical groups in both regions and does not force them to access a single region to perform analytics, greatly reducing the latency in accessing the data in the analytical store.

Before the analytical store was available, a common method to perform analytics against your data in Azure Cosmos DB was to use the *Apache Spark* connector. The Spark connector is a library for Apache Spark to connect to your Azure Cosmos DB account and ingest data into data frames for transformation and landing into a storage account. If you haven't worked with Spark before, it is a distributed big data processing engine. Using the Spark connector, however, consumes RUs. But the library introduces methods for limiting RU consumption in an attempt to reduce the impact to your transactional workload. The Spark connector does not interact with the analytical store and instead connects directly to your transactional store. Since the connector is accessing the transactional store, the data remains in its row format (JSON).

A benefit to accessing the transactional store is the data is in its native format of JSON, allowing the Spark connector to interact with the JSON document and its hierarchical structure, where the analytical store converts your JSON to a columnar format, benefiting common analytics scenarios such as aggregates but flattens the JSON document into columns. The Spark connector can also access data in real time since the connector does not have to wait for data to be converted into a columnar format and made available in the analytical store. Keep in mind, there is a distinction between using the Spark connector and using Spark to access the analytical store. The Spark connector can be used in any Spark cluster (open source Apache Spark, Databricks, Synapse Spark) which provides flexibility. When using Spark to access the analytical store, you must use Azure Synapse Spark by leveraging the Azure Synapse Link capabilities. This limits which service you can use but provides all the benefits of the analytical store. Synapse Spark supports Python, Scala, Spark SQL, .NET Spark, and SparkR.

Azure Synapse Link

Azure Synapse is Microsoft's flagship data analytics service. It provides a single pane of glass interface for data warehousing via SQL, SQL serverless pools, Kusto pools, and open source Apache Spark. The Synapse service also provides low-code ETL/ELT orchestration via Pipelines. Synapse can be considered the "center of gravity" for analytics in Azure providing all of the services data engineers and analysts need in one place. As such, Synapse also provides connectivity to other data services via Synapse Link.

Azure Synapse Link provides near real-time access to data stores such as Azure Cosmos DB, Azure SQL, and Dataverse. This access requires zero ETL to enable analytics, business intelligence, and machine learning. Azure Cosmos DB provides data access to Synapse Link via the analytical store where Azure SQL seamlessly exports data to Synapse dedicated SQL pools.

Synapse Link allows connections to your data by connecting to external data in Synapse. See Figure 11-1 to understand how to connect to Azure Cosmos DB analytical store in Synapse. The "Data" tab in Synapse is where connections to data sources like SQL, Azure Storage, and Azure Cosmos DB are managed. From this view, a SQL script leveraging SQL serverless or a Spark notebook can be used to interact with the data.

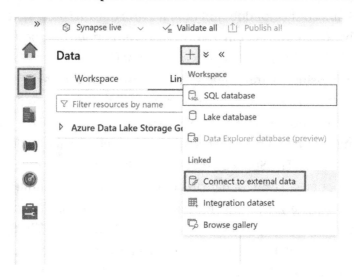

Figure 11-1. Connect to analytical store using Azure Synapse Link

Working with the Analytical Store

Before connecting to your Azure Cosmos DB account, we must enable Synapse Link on your account and the analytical store on your containers. Synapse Link can be enabled in the "features" blade in the Azure Portal for your Azure Cosmos DB account. A new experience has been provided for accounts using the NoSQL API where instead of enabling Synapse Link through the features blade, a new blade called "Azure Synapse Link" has been added. This updated experience makes it easier to manage which containers have the analytical store enabled. When creating a new container, an option will be presented to enable the analytical store for that container. This setting can be made after creation, but only for the NoSQL API (via the updated experience mentioned previously).

Once the connection is made to your Azure Cosmos DB account in Synapse, you will see the data source appear in the Data tab of your Azure Synapse workspace. If you don't see it immediately, refresh the page (Figure 11-2).

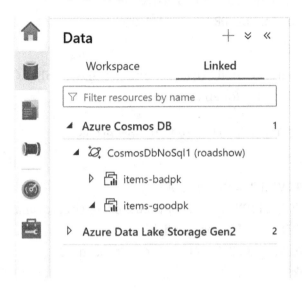

Figure 11-2. *Synapse Workspace External Data*

Under the Azure Cosmos DB account, you will see the containers listed. You can right-click any of these containers to create a new SQL script or create a Spark notebook. Let's start with a serverless SQL script.

Synapse Link for Serverless SQL

Synapse serverless SQL is an on-demand engine for performing analytics using T-SQL. In your Azure Synapse account, a serverless SQL pool is provided by default. When working with SQL scripts in the next steps, you will know you are using serverless if your "Connect to" tab of your SQL script says "Built-in." This represents the built-in serverless engine which requires no management. To get started, right-click the container you plan to query. A new SQL script will be loaded in the design view of Azure Synapse. But first, we need to create a credential for accessing the Azure Cosmos DB account. See Listing 11-1 for an example.

Listing 11-1. Create SQL Serverless Credential

```
CREATE CREDENTIAL [cosmos-nosql-1]
    WITH IDENTITY = 'SHARED ACCESS SIGNATURE',
    SECRET = '<your Cosmos DB account key>'
GO
```

Once the credential is created, we can submit a standard SELECT query to view the top 100 rows. See Listing 11-2 for an example.

Listing 11-2. SELECT Top 100 Using SQL Serverless

```
SELECT TOP 100 *
FROM OPENROWSET(PROVIDER = 'CosmosDB',
               CONNECTION = 'Account=cosmos-nosql;Database=roadshow',
               OBJECT = 'items-goodpk',
               SERVER_CREDENTIAL = 'cosmos-nosql-1'
) AS [items-goodpk]
```

After the preceding query is run, you will see a tabular representation of your data (Table 11-1).

Table 11-1. *Tabular Output*

zipCode	_rid	_etag	_ts	id	city
54988-0299	tz8WAOpgG02...	"7403177e-000...	1668099752	2fe9f4ec-a0e1-...	New Rhianna
63220-0577	tz8WAOpgG02...	"7403187e-000...	1668099752	e96c18c6-2216...	Torphyton
21112-2473	tz8WAOpgG02...	"7403197e-000...	1668099752	1a4432d6-57b8...	Port Dillon
56102	tz8WAOpgG02...	"74031a7e-000...	1668099752	16ee6be5-aa9a...	Robelton

By default, the NoSQL and Gremlin APIs leverage the *well-defined* schema representation. This is the simplest way to represent the data but comes with a drawback. The analytical store must convert a hierarchical structure into a flat one and convert data types. This can cause properties which do not conform to the proper data type conversions to be dropped from the analytical store. There is also a *full fidelity* schema representation (the default for the API for MongoDB). When using the full fidelity schema representation, data is presented as a key/value pair. The benefit over the well-defined schema representation is that no properties will be dropped or excluded regardless of data type issues. An example of the output of a full fidelity schema representation is provided in Table 11-2.

Table 11-2. *Representation of Full Fidelity Schema*

date_rep	cases	geo_id
{"date":"2020-08-13"}	{"int32":"254"}	{"string":"RS"}
{"date":"2020-08-12"}	{"int32":"235"}	{"string":"RS"}
{"date":"2020-08-11"}	{"int32":"316"}	{"string":"RS"}

Synapse Link for Synapse Spark

To get started using a Spark notebook, right-click your container and click "New notebook"➤ "load to dataframe". Spark is not a serverless service in Azure Synapse and requires you to create a cluster. If there is no cluster in your "Attach to" drop-down above your Spark notebook, click manage pools and create a pool. A small pool will be fine for this example. Use the Microsoft documentation to help you if you'd like to understand more about this process.

No changes are required to the provided boiled plate code (Listing 11-3) as compared to the serverless pool which required a credential. Simply click the play button to the left of the cell of code and wait for the results. The first time you run a cell against your cluster, the cluster will take a few minutes to power up.

Listing 11-3. Spark Notebook Using Synapse Link

```
df = spark.read\
    .format("cosmos.olap")\
    .option("spark.synapse.linkedService", "CosmosDbNoSql1")\
    .option("spark.cosmos.container", "items-goodpk")\
    .load()

display(df.limit(10))
```

The output will be the same as the serverless SQL pool output. Leveraging Spark and full featured, dynamic languages like Python provides a lot of functionality for data engineers.

In addition to reading the data, we can write the data back to Azure Cosmos DB using Spark. Doing this will impact the performance of the transactional store and consume RUs, since the data is being committed to the transactional store. This write activity can be performed on the same container or a different one. The amount of time the write activity takes will be based on the amount of data in your data frame. Listing 11-4 contains an example cell of writing to a new container.

Listing 11-4. Writing to a New Container Using Spark

```
df.write.format("cosmos.oltp")\
    .option("spark.synapse.linkedService", "CosmosDbNoSql1")\
    .option("spark.cosmos.container", "items-goodpk-new")\
    .mode('append')\
    .save()
```

Summary

Azure Cosmos DB is a hybrid transactional and analytical data platform. The analytical store provides seamless, zero ETL data access to your data in a columnar format. This greatly benefits analytics use cases as well as business intelligence and machine learning. The analytical store is enabled on an Azure Cosmos DB account and leveraged by Azure Synapse Analytics. Synapse supports accessing data via serverless SQL pools and Synapse Spark. These services provide data engineers with zero ETL access and transformations of your data using T-SQL, Python, Scala, .NET Spark, and others. As with other chapters, I highly recommend taking a look at the companion repository and reviewing the links provided.

CHAPTER 12

Design and Implement Change Feeds

An exciting and powerful feature of Azure Cosmos DB is the *change feed*. The change feed is similar to CDC (change data capture) in relational systems in that it provides a record of changes to a container in the order in which they occur. This functionality can come in handy in several key scenarios:

- Event-driven computing and notifications

- Real-time stream processing

- Data movement

- Event sourcing

As mentioned previously, there are trade-offs that come with the flexibility and performance offered by NoSQL data stores. The change feed can help address some of these trade-offs such as denormalization, referential integrity, aggregations, and data movement.

Modern developers look for functionality in their data store which can help meet the needs of their use case without burdening the architecture with additional services to deploy and maintain. The change feed removes the burden from the client of resolving downstream dependencies to the data it is producing while also replacing common architecture such as queues and pub/sub services that would be required to stream changes to other applications. The change feed is enabled by default and there is no cost to utilize it other than interacting with the documents and leases (more on this later). Change feed is supported for all APIs except the API for Table Storage.

© Steve Flowers 2023

S. Flowers, *Designing and Implementing Cloud-native Applications Using Microsoft Azure Cosmos DB*, Certification Study Companion Series, https://doi.org/10.1007/978-1-4842-9547-2_12

The goal of this chapter is to provide a strong understanding of what the change feed is, when you will want to use it, and how to implement it in your project. The DP-420 exam will expect the test taker to have a strong grasp on these mechanics of the change feed as well as the common properties and methods for implementing the change feed in your projects.

Common Change Feed Use Cases

Consider an e-commerce site which provides many products to consumers to browse and purchase. Based on our earlier discussions on data modeling, perhaps you have denormalized your data which represents the user's shopping cart. An example document describing a user's shopping cart may only contain a product name, price, and id to the full product details which reside in another document. This greatly improves the speed at which we can read and update the user's cart, but what happens when a product's name is changed or the price raises? How can we reconcile the inconsistent state of data that would arise from this scenario without forcing the client to do the work? The data model just described may look like in Listing 12-1.

Listing 12-1. Product/User Cart Denormalization Example

```
// Product Document
{
  "id" : "<guid>",
  "name" : "Widget Webcam model 2",
  "vendor" : "Widget Co.",
  "price" : "149.99"
}

// User Cart Document
{
  "id" : "<guid>",
  "name" : "Steve",
  "cart" : [
    {
      "productId" : "<productGuid>",
      "productPrice" : "149.99",
```

```
      "quantity" : 2
    }
  ]
}
```

If we think back to our time spent discussing data modeling, this data model represents a hybrid approach where some data has been embedded (product data embedded in the user cart) and some data is referenced. If our e-commerce application has a web interface for vendors to change the price of their products, during this process the product document would likely be updated to reflect the new price. But this leaves user cart documents with outdated data.

The change feed can listen to the "create" and "update" operations occurring on a specific container allowing you to execute code in reaction to those changes. In the case of our e-commerce application, if the price is updated on the product document and we are monitoring the change feed of the product container, we can then react to the change in price using an *Azure Function* or a custom process implementing the *change feed processor*.

Another common use case is to stream data from our applications for consumers who may want to transact and interact with our data such as APIs and streaming data processors. For instance, once an order is submitted in our e-commerce application, someone must fulfill the order and handle shipping to the customer. We could write an application that occasionally reads our container in batches and sends the data to another system which allows for fulfillment, but this would be a slow process. We could also rely on the client to, in parallel to submitting the order to the database, also submit the order to a message queue that is being consumed by an application for fulfillment. But this creates a lot of extra data consistency checks, exception handling, and additional services to maintain. The change feed eliminates the requirement that the client do any additional work to ship the data allowing a downstream producer to consume the change feed (much as they would a queue).

And as performance is typically our primary focus for using a NoSQL based data store, the change feed can help there as well. As discussed in previous chapters, aggregation is limited and can be challenging in NoSQL systems. Using the change feed, we can create and maintain our aggregates in their own document for high performant reads. Consider a competitive online video game which is tracking player points and team points as the game progresses. Players should be able to view player points and total team points at any time during the game. But providing these aggregates on-demand would be slow and computationally expensive. Instead as a player scores we can update a document that hosts the aggregates for our game. When a player scores, an event is produced which gets stored in a container. If we listen to that container using the change feed, we can then update a document containing our aggregates. See Listing 12-2 for an example data model.

Listing 12-2. Example Data Model of Aggregation

```
// Player Score Event Document
{
  "id" : "<guid>",
  "name" : "player1",
  "event" : "score"
}

// Match Scoreboard Aggregate Document
{
  "id" : "<guid>",
  "name" : "Match-1B123CxA0-EastUS",
  "team1Score" : 4,
  "team2Score" : 2,
  "team1" : [
    {
      "type" : "player",
      "id" : "player1",
      "score" : 3
    },
    {
      "type" : "player",
      "id" : "player2",
      "score" : 1
    }
  ]
...
```

As you can see, this is essentially a *materialized view* pattern which is common in the relational world. This is a common approach as our data is actually stored to disk for fast and performant retrieval. All that is needed is a processor listening to the change feed for the "score" events and, as they come in, updating the match scoreboard document.

Finally, the change feed can be used for data movement. If events entering Azure Cosmos DB containers need to be replicated to a pub/sub service like Azure Event Hubs or Service Bus, for instance, downstream processors can then consume events from a messaging service. You can also filter or transform the data and partition by replicating the data to specific Event Hubs. Using the change feed and a processor of the change feed, data could be integrated with many systems.

Other data movement scenarios include backup or migration. If you have long-term backup requirements that go beyond the limits of the built-in backup service, you can use the change feed to replicate data to a storage account for easy access. Migration scenarios may include moving your workload off of Azure Cosmos DB or making configuration changes which require a new container. For instance, if you've determine the partition key is incorrect for a container, you can't change the partition key and must create a new container. You can use the change feed to migrate all new data to the new container. The change feed allows you to start from any point of time, making migration easy.

Processing the Change Feed

Think of the change feed as a list of documents sorted by timestamp. As a document is inserted or updated, it is added to the top of the list. Inserted documents are straightforward; the new document will now be a new document in the change feed. Updated documents, however, are only represented by a single document. Unlike traditional CDC, we do not get a "chain of events" but what we get is the current state of the document sorted by its modified timestamp. This means that some intermediate changes may not be picked up when processing the change feed. If several updates occurred before you checked the change feed, you will only see the current state of the document – not the intermediate actions that lead to its current state. Let me provide a quick example to clarify what I mean.

1. *Document "A" is created with property "Name" set to "Sarah".*

2. *Read the change feed.*

3. *Document "A" "Name" property is updated from "Sarah" to "Steve".*

4. *Document "A" "Name" property is updated to "John".*

5. *Document "A" "Name" property is updated to "Steve".*

6. *Read the change feed.*

In this example, at step 2 when the change feed is read the new document will be present as expected and the value of the "Name" property is "Sarah". In steps 3-5 the document is updated three times. When the change feed is read at step 6, document "A" will have the value "Steve" for the "Name" property. The processing of the change feed is unaware to the fact that the "Name" property was ever "John". The change feed currently lacks support for intermediate updates between checks. This is important to understand as you interact with the change feed to understand what data you will receive.

So how do we interact with the change feed? The answer is the *change feed processor* (CFP). The CFP is part of the Azure Cosmos DB SDK which simplifies the process of reading the change feed and distributing processing across multiple change feed consumers. We define the container we wish to monitor, a lease container for keeping track of where we are in processing the change feed, and a compute instance which performs the processing.

The compute instance refers to whatever is running your code that is instantiating the CFP whether that be your local machine, a VM, or an app service. You can have multiple compute instances processing the same change feed at the same time to increase processing of the change feed. All compute that is monitoring the same container will share the same lease container so that all instances are aware of what data has been processed. The CFP for each compute instance will have the same *processorName* but be identified by a unique *WithInstanceName* as to identify each individual processor. The amount of scalability is determined by the number of physical partitions in your container. If your container has six physical partitions, you can have six change feed processors running at one time to process changes. Listing 12-3 shows an example of implementing the CFP in .NET.

Listing 12-3. C# Change Feed Processor Example

```
1    Container leaseContainer = cosmosClient.GetContainer(databaseName, leaseContainerName);
2
3    ChangeFeedProcessor changeFeedProcessor = cosmosClient.GetContainer(databaseName, sourceContainerName)
4        .GetChangeFeedProcessorBuilder<ToDoItem>(processorName: "changeFeedSample", onChangesDelegate: HandleChangesAsync)
5            .WithInstanceName("consoleHost")
6            .WithLeaseContainer(leaseContainer)
7            .Build();
```

As mentioned earlier in this chapter, you can start processing the change feed from any point in time. This can be accomplished by passing a date time to the *WithStartTime* builder extension in our change feed processor class object as shown in Listing 12-4. This includes starting at a specific point in time or from the lowest time possible of the documents in the container. To start from the beginning of a specific container's lifetime, pass `DateTime.MinValue.ToUniversalTime()` to *WithStartTime*.

Listing 12-4. C# Example of WithStartTime

```
1    Container leaseContainer = client.GetContainer(databaseId, Program.leasesContainer);
2
3    Container monitoredContainer = client.GetContainer(databaseId, Program.monitoredContainer);
4
5    ChangeFeedProcessor changeFeedProcessor = monitoredContainer
6        .GetChangeFeedProcessorBuilder<ToDoItem>("changeFeedTime", Program.HandleChangesAsync)
7            .WithInstanceName("consoleHost")
8            .WithLeaseContainer(leaseContainer)
9            .WithStartTime(particularPointInTime)
10           .Build();
11
```

Using Azure Functions

Implementing the change feed processor requires that you develop and operationalize the code to connect to the change feed. However, if you want a fast and low maintenance solution, Azure Functions have built-in integrations to Azure Cosmos DB that implement the change feed processor for you. For most use cases, this will be the right path to take as it reduces the amount of management that is required to maintain your service and allows you to focus on the code logic that is impactful to your use case.

Azure Functions is a serverless platform on Azure that allows you to focus on writing code and not maintaining infrastructure. They come with *bindings* which simplify the process of integrating with common Azure services such as Azure Cosmos DB. Azure Functions has a trigger binding, an input binding, and an output binding for Azure

Cosmos DB. The trigger binding refers to the implementation of a change feed processor which is handled for you. All you need to do is start writing the logic for processing changes. The input binding allows you to read documents and the output binding allows you to write documents but we'll focus on the trigger binding for now as it deals with the change feed.

The easiest way to get started is to click the "Add Azure Function" link in the "Integrations" blade from your Azure Cosmos DB account in the Azure Portal. You must provide the container you want to monitor, an Azure Function app, and the function language. In our case, we'll be exploring a C# script function app. I've chosen C# script for this portion as it is the quickest way to get started. Once completed, you will see a new function in your Azure Function app. The default code provided looks like Listing 12-5.

Listing 12-5. Default Azure Function for Azure Cosmos DB Trigger

```
1    #r "Microsoft.Azure.DocumentDB.Core"
2    using System;
3    using System.Collections.Generic;
4    using Microsoft.Azure.Documents;
5
6    public static void Run(IReadOnlyList<Document> input, ILogger log)
7    {
8        if (input != null && input.Count > 0)
9        {
10           log.LogInformation("Documents modified " + input.Count);
11           log.LogInformation("First document Id " + input[0].Id);
12       }
13   }
14
```

As you can see, the Run method has a parameter for *IReadOnlyList<Documents>*. This is the trigger that the wizard has configured for you. You can find the configuration in the *function.json* file or in the "Integration" tab. If you provide access to your Azure Cosmos DB account to this Function, as documents are added or updated in the monitored container, this Function will trigger. You can verify by looking at the "Monitor" tab of the Function, which will show the log output.

If you want to quickly and easily replicate documents to a new container for a migration, such as migrating to a new partition key, your function may look like Listing 12-6.

Listing 12-6. Azure Function Trigger Binding with Output Binding

```
1    #r "Microsoft.Azure.DocumentDB.Core"
2    #r "Newtonsoft.Json"
3
4    using System;
5    using System.Collections.Generic;
6    using Microsoft.Azure.Documents;
7    using Newtonsoft.Json.Linq;
8
9    public static void Run(IReadOnlyList<Document> input, out object outputDocument, TraceWriter log)
10   {
11       log.Verbose("Document count " + input.Count);
12       log.Verbose("First document Id " + input[0].Id);
13
14       dynamic doc = JObject.Parse(input[0].ToString());
15
16       log.Verbose("Name: " + doc.name);
17
18       outputDocument = new {
19           id = doc.id,
20           name = doc.name,
21           number = doc.number
22       };
23   }
```

This script leverages both the trigger binding which gets triggered on each update or create operation and the output binding which writes a document. The output binding is denoted by the "out object" named "outputDocument". We can extend this further such as calling a stored procedure which updates our aggregate document or assists with referential integrity.

Beyond the most basic scenarios, an Azure Function using C# scripts will be limited. At that point I suggest implementing an "in-process" Function, which you develop locally in your favorite IDE and deploy to your Azure Function. This brings a lot of "quality of life" improvements. As you perform more complicated logic, you will need to manage and implement your own Azure Cosmos DB client. The Azure Function still handles the bindings but you are free to organize and manage your code how you see fit. There is an example Function which has been authored using a local IDE in the companion repository for this book. It is too much code to include here but I highly recommend you review the project. Listing 12-7 shows a snippet from the code where a stored procedure is called to update a "task" document with the new name of a user.

Listing 12-7. Locally Developed Azure Function Calling a Stored Procedure

```
if (input != null && input.Count > 0)
{
    log.LogInformation("Documents modified " + input.Count);
    log.LogInformation("First document Id " + input[0].Id);

    Database database = client.GetDatabase("test-shared");
    Container container = database.GetContainer("task-tasks");

    foreach (Doc item in input){
        log.LogInformation($"Doc changed: {item.Name}");

        dynamic user = new System.Dynamic.ExpandoObject();
        user.name = item.Name;
        user.id = item.Id;

        var result = await container.Scripts.ExecuteStoredProcedureAsync<string>("updateTaskUser", new PartitionKey("task"), new[] {user});

        log.LogInformation(result);
    }

}
```

The *container.Scripts.ExecuteStoredProcedureAsync* handles passing our object to the stored procedure stored in our container. This provides a lot of flexibility as well as atomicity in working with data in our change feed.

Summary

In this chapter we discussed the Azure Cosmos DB Change Feed. The change feed allows us to interactively work with changes to documents in our containers. This enables common use cases such as event-based patterns, data movement like backup and migration, and implementing data integrity patterns. Almost every project using Azure Cosmos DB that I have been involved in leverages the change feed in one way or another. It is a critical component of applications and will be an important feature to understand for the exam. As with other chapters, I highly recommend that you work with the change feed before taking the exam. Understand how to read the change feed using both the change feed processor and an Azure Function. Play around with the scenarios provided in this chapter. It will help cement in your memory the procedure for properly leveraging the change feed.

CHAPTER 13

Implement Solutions Across Services

When taking the DP-420 exam, it is important to not only have a deep understanding of the inner workings of Azure Cosmos DB, but to also understand how Azure Cosmos DB integrates with other services in a production environment. This includes having familiarity with additional Azure services that are often integrated with Azure Cosmos DB.

After completing this chapter, it is important to be familiar with, at a basic level, what these services are and what function they often serve in modern application architecture. The services covered in this chapter will include Azure Event Hubs, Azure Functions, and Azure Cognitive Search. To successfully answer case study questions, you must be able to answer the following questions:

- What service provides pub/sub functionality for message streaming?

- How can messages from a stream be easily written to Azure Cosmos DB?

- How can you perform full text search over Azure Cosmos DB documents and when would this be useful?

To illustrate how you must think about an architecture that includes Azure Cosmos DB, we will walk through an example architecture from end to end. Through the example architecture, you should gain an understanding of the potential for integration with Azure Cosmos DB, how the services connect almost seamlessly, and how to deploy similar patterns in your production environments.

© Steve Flowers 2023
S. Flowers, *Designing and Implementing Cloud-native Applications Using Microsoft Azure Cosmos DB*,
Certification Study Companion Series, https://doi.org/10.1007/978-1-4842-9547-2_13

Event-Driven Architecture

Modern applications often implement event-driven patterns. Services which need to communicate the progress or status of processing data place messages on an event stream (pub/sub) or a message queue for downstream consumers. The messages are often represented in JSON format. In a pub/sub model, one or many consumers may be subscribed to the event stream and perform independent work on the data that is consumed.

Azure Cosmos DB meets the needs of modern application developers as many event-driven patterns can be enabled by built-in functionality such as the Change Feed. Leveraging the power of tightly integrated services like Azure Event Hubs and Azure Functions, event-driven patterns are unlocked when using Azure Cosmos DB as your data store. The example we will be walking through in this chapter is presented in Figure 13-1.

Figure 13-1. *Event-Driven Architecture with Azure Cosmos DB*

Let's step through this diagram to understand what is going on. In step 1, a client application or service places a message (event) on an Azure Event Hub acting as a producer. Azure Event Hubs stores these messages and allows one or many consumers to read these messages. Event Hubs defines "consumer groups," which provide a unique checkpoint for each consumer to track which messages have been read.

Azure Cosmos DB cannot act as a consumer of messages on an Event Hub so we need a service to act as an intermediary. In this case, Azure Functions is an excellent choice as it is a serverless PaaS offering, which provides simple integration with Azure Cosmos DB. As discussed in the previous chapter, Azure Functions have built-in bindings for several services. The Azure Function can be automatically triggered by a batch of messages from Azure Event Hubs. Once the Azure Function is triggered, an output binding for Azure Cosmos DB can be used to write the messages to an Azure Cosmos DB container (step 3).

As discussed in the data modeling and other chapters of this book, denormalization is common, and though data from our stream has been written to a container in Azure Cosmos DB, we may have cause to also load that data into another container. Whether the use case requirements are to create a second data model for faster reading or a materialized view pattern for aggregation, we can use the Azure Cosmos DB Change Feed. In step 4, we have new documents placed in the change feed and triggering an Azure Function in step 5.

Step 6 is where we are performing an aggregation for a materialized view pattern or copying documents to a new container with a different partition key to serve a different access pattern. We may also be using the Change Feed, as discussed in the previous chapter, to denormalize our data or ensure referential integrity. In the next section, we will walk through implementing this event-driven pattern.

Implement the Event-Driven Architecture

First, we need to create an Azure Event Hub to send data to. Using the Azure Marketplace, search for Event Hubs to create a new resource. The basic requirements for a new Event Hub (EH) are as follows:

- Subscription

- Resource group

- Namespace name

- Region

- Pricing tier

- Throughput units

For this example, the basic pricing tier will suffice with one throughput unit. There are some differences that won't affect this simple use case but the limits for the basic tier are as follows:

- 256 KB max message size

- 1 consumer group

- 100 brokered connections

- 1-day retention max

Depending on when you read this text, tiers may have changed.

This is just to list a few. For dev/test this is fine but for production I would recommend standard or premium. We have created an Event Hubs *namespace* but we still need to create a hub. A namespace is a logical container for one-to-many hubs and the hubs are where we actually send our messages.

In the Azure Portal, select our new Event Hubs namespace and navigate to the Entities ➤ Event Hubs blade. Here we can create a new Event Hub. For now, just name the hub and click "Review + create". And finally, within the newly created Hub, click "Shared Access Policies" and create a new policy. We'll select "Send" and "Listen". This SAS policy will contain the connection string for our client.

Once the Event Hub has been created, we can use the .NET library **Azure. Messaging.EventHubs** to send and receive messages to the EH. I won't cover all of the particulars for creating a console application in .NET as it is outside of the scope of this book. However, there is a very good quick start on Microsoft Learn. Most importantly, I want to show the relevant code to send a batch of messages to your EH. Listing 13-1 provides an example.

Listing 13-1. Example Event Hub Client in .NET

```
EventHubProducerClient producerClient = new EventHubProducerClient(
    "<CONNECTION_STRING>",
    "<HUB_NAME>");

using EventDataBatch eventBatch = await producerClient.CreateBatchAsync();

for (int i = 1; i <= numOfEvents; i++)
```

```
{
    eventBatch.TryAdd(new EventData(Encoding.UTF8.GetBytes($"Event {i}")))
{

await producerClient.SendAsync(eventBatch);
```

As you can see from the example code, we create a *producerClient* and an *eventBatch* to then load our events to. Afterward, we use *producerClient.SendAsync(eventBatch)* to send our batch to the EH service. The *producerClient* in this example is using the connection string to connect. We need the name of our Hub (not namespace) and the connection string to connect. The quick start URL referenced will be included in the companion git repository for this chapter.

Next, we need an Azure Function to process these messages. We'll create a new Azure Function and then configure the input binding (EH) and the output binding (Azure Cosmos DB). Search the marketplace for "Function App" and create a new resource. The information we will need is

- Subscription

- Resource Group

- Function App Name

- Publish method (select Code for now)

- Runtime Stack (.NET)

- Version (6)

- Region

- Operating System (Windows)

- Plan Type (Consumption/Serverless)

We will also need to identify an Azure Storage account – either create a new one or use an existing one in your environment. Click Review + create to complete the configuration.

Now that we have a new Function App, we need to create a Function. The Function App is the host for one or many Functions within it. Navigate to the Functions blade in your Function App. Click "Create" to create a new Function. For simplicity's sake, select the portal for your development environment. And for the template, select Azure

Event Hub trigger. You will be asked to create a connection to your Event Hub. Select the appropriate EH and EH SAS policy. Change the Event Hub name to your hub name and leave the $Default consumer group.

Once the Function is created, you can navigate to the "Integrations" plane to see the data flow. There is a trigger, your function, and an output (which has not been defined yet). You Function's integration pane should look like Figure 13-2.

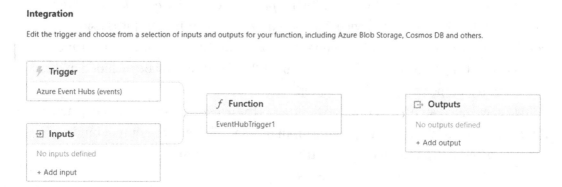

Figure 13-2. *Azure Function Integrations Pane*

In this configuration, the Function will be triggered by an EH batch and log each message as it arrives using the out-of-box default code.

To create the output to Azure Cosmos DB, click "Add output" in the Integrations pane. Set the following details:

- *Binding Type*: Azure Cosmos DB.

- *Cosmos DB account connection*: Create new.

- *Document parameter name*: outputDocument.

- *Database name*: Select a database in an Azure Cosmos DB NoSQL account.

- *Collection name*: Select a collection or create a new one.

- *If true, create the database and collection*: Yes if you want the Function to create the database and collection for you.

- Partition key is optional.

The "Document parameter name" identifies the object you will interact with to output messages to the Azure Cosmos DB container. Writing to your Azure Cosmos DB container becomes as easy as defining this object such as in Listing 13-2.

Listing 13-2. Azure Function Output Document

```
outputDocument = new {
    id = event.id,
    name = event.name,
    number = event.number
};
```

Now that data is flowing into your Azure Cosmos DB container, a great number of possibilities become available. As we discussed in the last chapter, we can leverage the Change Feed to trigger Azure Functions on newly inserted or updated documents. The Change Feed can trigger Azure Functions, which create aggregates, materialized views, or send the data elsewhere via a separate Azure Event Hub.

Azure Cognitive Search

The last integration we will discuss in this chapter is the integration of Azure Cognitive Search with your Azure Cosmos DB account. Azure Cognitive Search is a service which provides APIs and tools for building a rich search experience over your data. It supports full text search, fuzzy search, and indexing with lexical analysis. The service will load your data and perform indexing on top of it to make it searchable and easily scannable. We can then query this indexed data and perform semantic search on top of it.

Cognitive Search is great for adding typical search functionality to a web app such as an e-commerce application. It is purpose built to serve search results in a low-latency manner and can consolidate your heterogeneous data into a private, user-defined search index. Consider an e-commerce application with hundreds of thousands of vendors. To provide this list to your UI, you would need to query your documents to retrieve vendor names. You could also create documents that can store just a simple list of vendor names (denormalization) and reading that list may be fast but updating it to maintain referential integrity would be costly. A search index can remove the cost and complexity of serving this workload pattern.

An additional design pattern is focused on delivering point reads. As mentioned in previous chapters, a point read is the most efficient read operation. But the requirements for a point read are that you must know the partition key, and you must also know the id of the document. There are times when we don't have one or either of these pieces of information. IDs are often programmatically generated GUIDs. Partition keys are more likely to be known but perhaps you have the ID and not the partition key. By not having your partition key, you will be performing a fan-out query which, as you know from reading this book, is the most expensive form of query.

By importing and indexing your documents into Azure Cognitive Search, a query can be performed against the indexed data in search to provide the data required for a point read. For instance, if you know the name of a vendor but not the ID, it is much simpler to query Cognitive Search for the ID to assist your point read than perform a filter on your query (especially if your logical partition is large). Once you have retrieved the ID from Cognitive Search, you can run your point read. There are other times where perhaps your data is bifurcated: some data resides in Azure Cosmos DB and some in Azure SQL or Azure Storage. Azure Cognitive Search allows you to quickly ingest and index this data for use in your application.

Summary

When implementing Azure Cosmos DB for a use case, there will always be accompanying services that integrate with your database. The Azure ecosystem provides tightly integrated services which can be set up quickly to provide these integrations. We explored an event-driven design in this chapter, but there are many use cases where Azure Functions and Azure Cosmos DB will be deployed together and integrate other services and data streams. This chapter illustrates the importance of not only knowing how Azure Cosmos DB fits into your use case, but how to interact with the database using common PaaS services in the Azure ecosystem.

CHAPTER 14

Define and Implement an Indexing Strategy

Indexing is an important aspect of any database system. Indexes allow us to map the paths to data values to avoid scanning entire tables or containers for the information we need. Without an index, a query which is searching for all products from a specific vendor in a container would need to scan the entire container to return the data. With proper indexing, we can tell the engine where to find a specific vendor or a range of products while greatly reducing the latency and computational power required to complete our query.

In this chapter we will be covering how indexing in Azure Cosmos DB operates and what considerations are required to determine the appropriate indexing strategy. There are three types of indexes: range, spatial, and composite. It is important to understand when to use each type of index and what impact indexing has on your workload. Finally, it is important to understand how to implement indexes and measure their impact to performance on your workload.

Indexes in Azure Cosmos DB

There are three types of indexes offered in Azure Cosmos DB: *range*, *spatial*, and *composite*. When using the NoSQL API, every property is indexed by default. This allows developers to focus on their application while gaining the benefit of automatic indexing. However, a purposeful approach should be taken to your indexes before moving to production. It is important to understand how your data is modeled and accessed when evaluating your approach to indexing.

127

© Steve Flowers 2023
S. Flowers, *Designing and Implementing Cloud-native Applications Using Microsoft Azure Cosmos DB*, Certification Study Companion Series, https://doi.org/10.1007/978-1-4842-9547-2_14

Before we discuss the different types of indexes, let's talk about the benefits. Indexing provides a pointer to properties in your documents to prevent the database engine from having to scan every document in your container. Indexes are created and updated during write operations. They account for disk storage in your account, and while disk storage is inexpensive, it is good practice to monitor your index size. Indexes benefit your read operations represented as queries. The index allows the database engine to quickly retrieve documents that match your query predicates without having to evaluate every single document. This is important to understand, as indexing impacts your write performance and cost. If your workload is write intensive, like IoT telemetry or streaming events, you may not want to index your data or ensure your index is as small as possible. Conversely, if you have a read-intensive workload with complex queries and filtering, indexing is incredibly important to ensure high performance. Keep in mind having too many indexes can slow down writes.

When you create a new collection, it will come with a default indexing policy. The policy will look like Listing 14-1.

Listing 14-1. Default Indexing Policy

```
{
    "indexingMode": "consistent",
    "automatic": true,
    "includedPaths": [
        {
            "path": "/*"
        }
    ],
    "excludedPaths": [
        {
            "path": "/\"_etag\"/?"
        }
    ]
}
```

First, the indexing mode is *consistent*. This means that the index will be updated synchronously as you create, update, or delete documents. If this is set to *none*, then indexing is disabled on this container. The *automatic* property dictates that Azure

Cosmos DB will index items as they are written automatically. Next, we have both the *includedPaths* and *excludedPaths* properties. The included paths are the paths that represent the hierarchy of our JSON data that will be indexed. As you can see, the default indexing policy indexes every property in our documents automatically and synchronously using a wildcard statement.

Excluded paths do the opposite: paths added here will not be indexed. If you plan to only include one or two paths in your index, it is easier to exclude the root path and include the more specific paths that you do want indexed in the "includedPaths". If you plan to exclude only a few properties, it is easier to include the root path and exclude the specific paths. Regardless of which method you choose, the root path must be present in either the include or exclude path policy. Precedence for include versus exclude is given to the most specific path. For example, `"/user_profile/*"` takes precedence over `"/*"`.

As mentioned, a default indexing policy is included automatically. You can find the indexing policy for a container by navigating to the Data Explorer pane in your Azure Cosmos DB account. In the settings for your container, you will see the tab "Index Policy". If your indexing policy is improperly formatted, an error will occur when you attempt to save. Once saved, your queries will automatically use the new indexes.

The examples we've looked at so far include a wildcard, meaning any element below the configured path. However, we also have access to the "?" identifier which indicates a scalar value (a string or a number) and the "[]" identifier which represents arrays. As an example, if our "user_profile" includes name, address, employee_id, and phone number, we can represent the scalar value of employee_id as `"/user_profile/employee_id/?"`.

Range, Spatial, and Composite Indexes

Range indexes are the most basic. The default indexing policy is a range index. Range indexes are based on an ordered hierarchy, that is, the hierarchy of a JSON document. Some examples of range indexes are as follows:

- `/*`
- `/user_profile/employee_id/?`
- `/user_profile/addresses/[]`
- `/user_profile/addresses/[]/city/?`

Range indexes are best used for equality, matching, ranges, order by, and join queries. Order by queries must have a range index if ordering by a single property. A composite index is required when ordering by more than one property. Here are some example queries from Microsoft documentation that are best for range indexes.

Listing 14-2. Example Queries for a Range Index

```
SELECT * FROM container c WHERE c.property = 'value'
SELECT * FROM c WHERE ARRAY_CONTAINS(c.tags, "tag1")
SELECT * FROM c WHERE IS_DEFINED(c.property)
SELECT * FROM c WHERE CONTAINS(c.property, "value")
SELECT * FROM container c ORDER BY c.property
SELECT child FROM container c JOIN child IN c.properties WHERE child
= 'value'
```

Composite indexes are much more efficient when performing filtering on more than one field. These indexes are beneficial for queries including predicates such as in an "Order By" or "Where" clause. When creating the composite index, we include the path to the property as well as the order *ascending* or *descending*. An example composite index looks like the example in Listing 14-3.

Listing 14-3. Composite Index Example

```
{
    "automatic":true,
    "indexingMode":"Consistent",
    "includedPaths":[
        {
            "path":"/*"
        }
    ],
    "excludedPaths":[],
    "compositeIndexes":[
        [
            {
                "path":"/user_profile/lastname",
                "order":"ascending"
```

```
        }
    ]
  ]
}
```

As you'll notice in the example, there is no wildcard or scalar ("?") representation in the composite index. This is because there is an implicit "/?" at the end of each statement in a composite index. Additionally, it is important that your "order" matches the order of your query. If your query is ascending, make sure your composite index is also ascending.

```
SELECT * FROM c ORDER BY c.user_profile.name ASC
```

Equality queries can also be optimized using a composite index. For example, if we want to write a query where we search for all employees named "Steve" who are over the age of 64, a composite query will help us. The query may look like the as follows:

```
SELECT * FROM c WHERE c.user_profile.name = "Steve" AND c.age > 64
```

A composite index with the "/user_profile/age" property ordered by ascending will be much faster than a standard range index. The engine will be able to quickly jump to the age range of 64 and above, skipping all of the lower values in the index.

Finally, spatial indexes help improve the performance of our queries for spatial data like geometry or geography. An example spatial index from the Microsoft documentation is represented in Listing 14-4.

Listing 14-4. Example Spatial Index

```
{
    "indexingMode": "consistent",
    "automatic": true,
    "includedPaths": [
        {
            "path": "/*"
        }
    ],
    "excludedPaths": [
        {
```

```
            "path": "/_etag/?"
        }
    ],
    "spatialIndexes": [
        {
            "path": "/path/to/geojson/property/?",
            "types": [
                "Point",
                "Polygon",
                "MultiPolygon",
                "LineString"
            ]
        }
    ]
}
```

There are four possible types for a spatial index:

- Point

- Polygon

- MultiPolygon

- LineString

Queries that leverage the spatial index would include keywords such as ST_ DISTANCE, ST_WITHIN, and ST_INTERSECTS. ST_DISTANCE tells us the distance between two geometric points. This can be very useful for apps which leverage a map and direct the user on the shortest path between two places of interest. ST_WITHIN tells of if the first parameter of a spatial expression is contained within the second. This can be beneficial for real estate applications determining whether or not an address resides in a specific neighborhood or district.

Monitoring Index Usage

As we add indexes to our containers in Azure Cosmos DB, we could assume they are working as expected, but that is not very scientific. We really want to make sure that our indexes are serving our queries and that we have empirical proof of their impact on performance. There are two ways to quickly gain the information you need on index usage: Data Explorer for a graphical experience or the SDK for a programmatic experience.

In the Data Explorer query window, we can examine the Query Stats to determine the RU cost and index usage of a query. Take a look in Figure 14-1 for an example of a properly indexed query.

```
5    select * from c where c.country = "Chile"
6
```

Results   **Query Stats**

METRIC	VALUE
ⓘ Request Charge	14.74 RUs
ⓘ Showing Results	1 - 100
ⓘ Retrieved document count	200
ⓘ Retrieved document size	135922 bytes
ⓘ Output document count	200
ⓘ Output document size	136222 bytes
ⓘ Index hit document count	200
ⓘ Index lookup time	0.67 ms
ⓘ Document load time	1.1700000000000002 ms

Figure 14-1. *Index Usage in Query Stats*

We can see right away that the RU charge is quite low. The index hit 200 documents and the index lookup time was 0.67 milliseconds. Now let's look at a similar query that has not been indexed in Figure 14-2.

```
12    select * from c where c.city = "Jaclynfort"
13
14
```

Results   **Query Stats**

Query Statistics

METRIC	VALUE
ⓘ Request Charge	172395.07999999996 RUs
ⓘ Showing Results	1 - 54
ⓘ Retrieved document count	10550063
ⓘ Retrieved document size	7226638703 bytes
ⓘ Output document count	54
ⓘ Output document size	38505 bytes
ⓘ Index hit document count	0
ⓘ Index lookup time	0 ms
ⓘ Document load time	38364.810000000005 ms

Figure 14-2. *Large Query with No Index*

As you can see, the RU cost is 172 thousand! This is a similar query over the same container of just over 10 million documents. All documents were retrieved to complete the query, whereas in Figure 14-1, only the 200 matching documents were retrieved. We can see that no documents were hit by the index and the index lookup time was zero.

This method is great for testing, but we can get more prescriptive guidance from the SDK. This is a request option in the *FeedIterator<>* class called *PopulateIndexMetrics*, which I have provided example code for in Listing 14-5.

Listing 14-5. PopulateIndexMetrics in the SDK

```
using FeedIterator<User> filteredFeed = container.
GetItemQueryIterator<User>(
    queryDefinition: parameterizedQuery,
    requestOptions: new QueryRequestOptions
    {PopulateIndexMetrics = true});
```

By setting this option to "true", we can return the index metrics from our *FeedResponse<>* like in Listing 14-6.

Listing 14-6. FeedResponse Index Metrics

```
FeedResponse<User> response = await filteredFeed.ReadNextAsync();
Console.WriteLine(response.IndexMetrics);
```

The response property of *IndexMetrics* looks like as follows:

```
Index Utilization Information
  Utilized Single Indexes
    Index Spec: /country/?
    Index Impact Score: High
  Potential Single Indexes
  Utilized Composite Indexes
  Potential Composite Indexes
```

It outlines which indexes were used, in this case "/country/?" and the impact score for that index. Here we can see that the impact of this index is high. If we look at our un-indexed query, the index metrics are as follows:

```
Index Utilization Information
  Utilized Single Indexes
  Potential Single Indexes
    Index Spec: /city/?
    Index Impact Score: High
    ---
  Utilized Composite Indexes
  Potential Composite Indexes
```

The database engine is recommending a range index on the "city" property and the impact, as we know from our testing, would be very high.

Finally, we can use the Insights pane in our Azure Cosmos DB account to monitor overall metrics usage. In your Azure Cosmos DB account, open Insights from the navigation pane. Select a database and a container. On the "overview" page, there is a bird's eye line chart of the data usage and index usage. As you can see from Figure 14-3, the index is not being used by my example account.

Figure 14-3. *Insights on Index Usage*

Summary

Proper indexing is critical to the performance of your application. At scale, proper indexing not only translates to latency in your queries but the total cost for your workload. In the example provided, our indexed query was 1,000 more cost-effective than our un-indexed query. Azure Cosmos DB provides the tools needed to evaluate your queries and the benefit of indexing. Use the *IndexMetrics* in the SDK for indexing recommendations during testing to ensure you are implementing the most impactful indexes. And be prepared to address indexing on the DP-420 exam.

## CHAPTER 15

Monitor and Troubleshoot an Azure Cosmos DB Solution

Proper monitoring is critical for any application and helps you understand the health and utilization of your database service. Like most data services, Azure Cosmos DB has a *control plane* and a *data plane* that manages and executes activity against the service. The control plane includes activities used to control your service such as adding new databases and containers or setting throughput. The data plane includes any activity related to the data stored in the account such as reads, writes, queries, and deletions.

It is imperative to have a monitoring and alerting strategy for both the control plane and the data plane. In Azure Cosmos DB, we can configure the *diagnostic setting* for the account and determine which logs we capture and where to send them. Monitoring costly queries based on their RU consumption or alerting on failed transactions will enable you to optimize your solution and avoid costly downtime. It is important to understand what kind of activity is captured in each log type and how you can leverage this data for auditing your environment. A common approach is to send log data to Azure Monitor Log Analytics, or if you already have an enterprise logging solution, how to integrate the Azure Cosmos DB logs with a third-party solution.

In this chapter we will review the ways to monitor your Azure Cosmos DB workloads. Metrics are constantly emitted which will allow you to react to poor conditions whether it be latency, storage increases, or return codes. Additionally, we will explore the logging available to you which can be used to understand your workload and optimize performance of your application.

© Steve Flowers 2023
S. Flowers, *Designing and Implementing Cloud-native Applications Using Microsoft Azure Cosmos DB*, Certification Study Companion Series, https://doi.org/10.1007/978-1-4842-9547-2_15

Diagnostic Setting

Your Azure Cosmos DB account has a "Monitoring" group listed in the portal navigation pane. This is where your monitoring journey will start. The diagnostic settings pane allows you to configure which logs you'd like to capture and where those logs should be sent. Capturing logs allows for querying and alerting. You may write queries to determine the number of write operations or the cost of those operations. You may monitor status codes returned to your database. Whatever the case, it is important to ship these logs somewhere for analysis.

Once you open the diagnostic settings pane, you can add a new diagnostic setting. This allows you to treat logs from different sources differently from one another. Perhaps control plane logs should be sent to Azure Monitor Logs and data plane logs sent to Event Hub to be ingested into Splunk or another service. If you click "Add diagnostic setting", you are provided with options to control your logging flow. Other than providing this setting with a name, you will be confronted with a choice of logs and a choice of destinations.

The destination details are just that: where do you want logs to go? First, consider what your enterprise is using for centralized logging. If you use Azure Monitor Logs, then select "Send to Log Analytics workspace" and use your Log Analytics workspace (LAW) to query and define alerts. You can also send logs to an Azure Storage account or Azure Event Hub. Azure Event Hub is a popular destination for companies who are using a third-party logging tool like Splunk or Elk stack. These tools have plug-ins for ingesting logs from Azure Event Hub. This provides a lot of flexibility for organizations in defining their logging strategy.

The selection of logs will be determined by the API you have chosen for your Azure Cosmos DB account. If you have selected the NoSQL API, you don't need to log for "MongoRequests" or "TableApiRequests" so it is important to understand the data the various logs provide.

- *DataPlaneRequest*: Monitor CRUD operations for NoSQL API.

- *MongoRequests*: Monitor CRUD operations for API for Mongo.

- *CassandraRequests*: Monitor CRUD operations for API for Cassandra.

- *GremlinRequests*: Monitor CRUD operations for API for Gremlin.

- *QueryRuntimeStatistics*: Monitor queries, their partition key range, and query text (optional).

- *PartitionKeyStatistics*: Monitor query partition key range and storage to determine storage skew.

- *PartitionKeyRUConsumption*: Monitor query request charge (RU).

- *ControlPlaneRequests*: Logs creating of account, regions, databases, containers.

- *TableApiRequests*: Monitor CRUD operations for API for Table Storage.

When leveraging logs like "MongoRequests" or "TableApiRequests", it is not required to also log "DataPlaneRequests" as they apply to their respective APIs. You may decide, by configuring additional settings, to log "ControlPlaneRequests" to a LAW and "DataPlaneRequests" to Azure Event Hubs. Control plane logs, data plane logs, and query statistics are logs you likely want to always capture to monitor and support your application. Logs for partition key statistics and partition key consumption would only be captured if you are investigating a particular issue. This allows you to cut down on the logging noise and cost of additional storage.

Response Status Codes and Failure Metrics

The "DataPlaneRequests" logs will help you identify common issues when performing CRUD operations against the data store. These are some of the most valuable logs since they describe the success or failure of your client's interactions with Azure Cosmos DB. It is important to understand the response status codes that are returned to your application and configure alerts to reduce the time to remediate common issues.

Azure Cosmos DB implements HTTP status codes for clients performing operations against the data store. It is important to know which status codes are common for successful operations and which status codes could indicate an issue that should be investigated. Most of the status codes are common specifications for HTTP operations and some are specific to the operation of Azure Cosmos DB.

- **200 – *OK***: A CRUD operation was successful.

- **201 – *Created***: A POST operation created an item.

- **400 – *Bad Request***: The headers or body of the request were invalid.

- **401 – *Unauthorized*.**

- **408** – *Request timeout*: The request did not complete in the allotted time.

- **429** – *Too many requests*: Throughput limit has been exceeded.

Many of these are common status codes returned from any service. However, an important status code returned from Azure Cosmos DB is "429". If the number of requests exceeds the provisioned throughput for a database or container, a "429" is returned. For example, if your container is configured with 4,000 RUs at 90% average consumption, and a client attempts to insert millions of documents in a batch operation, some may succeed but eventually your container will run out of RUs. When there are no more RUs to service an operation, the client receives a "429" response. As mentioned in previous chapters, the SDK will retry automatically. Otherwise, the request will fail.

To optimize the cost of our solution, we don't want to add excessive throughput. While this would avoid the issue of "429" response codes and prevent operations from succeeding, it also creates a lot of cost overhead. Since the SDK will retry requests automatically, a small number of "429" responses is acceptable as long as they are retried successfully. Typically, the recommendation is 1–5% of operations can experience a "429" without affecting the success of your operations. More than 5%, however, means you should probably increase the throughput of your database or container.

Monitoring Insights

The Insights pane in your Azure Cosmos DB account provides a collection of reports to help you understand the current state of your account, databases, and containers. This is likely the first place to visit when experiencing issues or evaluating performance and optimization. As Figure 15-1 demonstrates, you can access metrics from the Insights blade and filter metrics based on date and time or database. You can configure the time range for the dashboard to either view macro-trends over time or zoom in on a particular point of time such as a bulk data load. You can also filter by database and container, allowing precision analysis of your workload.

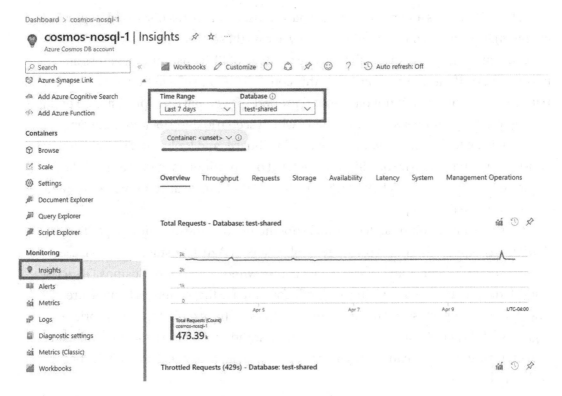

Figure 15-1. *Monitoring Insights Overview*

The overview page provides the most commonly beneficial metrics for understanding your Azure Cosmos DB account. *Total Requests* provides the count of all requests, that is, reads, writes, queries, deletes, and replace. This is an at-a-glance view of all the operations occurring in your account. The *Requests* tab of the dashboard allows you to dive further into this data, providing the count of various status codes like "200" and "429" and request operations by type like queries, reads, and writes.

The *Data and Index Usage* report on the overview tab tracks your data storage over time as well as your index usage. Use this report to determine the rate at which your data is growing, tracking large delete or TTL operations, and tracking the storage footprint of your indexes. To gain further insights, navigate to the *Storage* tab of your dashboard to also see the trend of document count and a breakdown of database/container data usage, index usage, and document count.

Finally, the overview page provides a report for *normalized RU consumption (max)*. This is a metric that is very important and sometimes confusing. Azure Cosmos DB scales horizontally, which means for high throughput accounts there are many logical partition keys and many physical partitions. Our goal (as discussed in previous chapters) is to spread our operations evenly across these partitions. The normalized RU consumption metric shows the max percentage of RU consumption across all partition keys. If this metric is at 100%, this could mean one of two things: you have a hot partition, and your data is not partitioned properly or you have not provisioned enough throughput for your needs. To understand which scenario describes your current state, navigate to the *Throughput* tab of the dashboard, and look at the normalized RU consumption heat map by partition range ID. If one partition is maxed at 100% but others are much lower, you have a hot partition. If they are all at 100%, you may need to provision more throughput.

There is some additional detail that is not included in the overview page. The *Availability* report will show you the reliability of your Azure Cosmos DB service. If Microsoft experiences an issue at a data center where your Azure Cosmos DB account is located, your availability will be affected. You can use these metrics to measure availability during an issue and in the future after you have added the appropriate high availability configuration to your account. Additional regions add cost but using availability metrics you can show leadership empirical evidence that justifies the additional expense.

The *Latency* tab in the dashboard will help you understand how long it is taking for Azure Cosmos DB to serve your workload. You can quickly view the server-side latency of all your configured regions. This can be very helpful in multi-region accounts where one region may be experiencing issues that other regions are not experiencing. Using this report, you can also see the clear difference in implementing gateway mode versus direct connection mode. These reports allow you to measure the difference in clients implementing different connection modes and may be a driver prioritizing changes with management. Finally, you can measure the latency by operation types such as read, write, and query. Figure 15-2 displays the server-side latency for a database which also denotes the type of operation: delete, query, read, write, and so on.

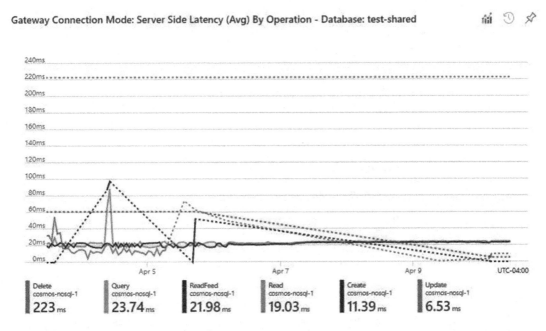

Figure 15-2. *Monitoring Insights Latency Report*

Querying Logs and Configuring Alerts

Querying Azure Cosmos DB logs in an Azure Log Analytics workspace (LAW) allows you to explore and investigate control plane and data plane operations in your Azure Cosmos DB account. Where metrics provided in the Insights pane of the portal allow you to quickly view trends and identify issues, the logs allow you to investigate specific issues, measure KPIs, and create alerts on common problems.

As discussed earlier in this chapter, through the diagnostic settings we can ship logs to Azure Monitor Logs by choosing a Log Analytics workspace as our target. Log Analytics is a separate service which must be created before you can ingest logs from Azure Cosmos DB. Once logs have been sent to a LAW, by selecting the scope of logs as your Azure Cosmos DB account, you will see the tables available for querying, as shown in Figure 15-3.

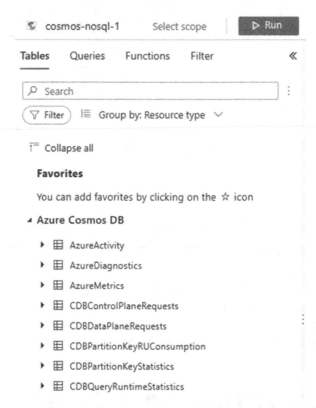

Figure 15-3. *Log Analytics Workspace*

These tables relate to the log selection in the Azure Cosmos DB account diagnostic settings. To query the logs, we must use KQL (Kusto Query Language), which is found throughout the Azure Monitor ecosystem. It is a very simple and intuitive language. Listing 15-1 is an example KQL query listing all of the data plane requests over the past seven days that were queried.

Listing 15-1. Example KQL Query

```
CDBDataPlaneRequests
| where TimeGenerated > ago(7d)
| where OperationName == "Query"
| project TimeGenerated, AccountName, RequestCharge, DurationMs
```

Figure 15-4 shows the output of that query.

TimeGenerated [UTC]	AccountName	RequestCharge	DurationMs
> 4/9/2023, 1:16:07.515 PM	COSMOS-NOSQL-1	2.83	2.3457
> 4/9/2023, 1:16:17.781 PM	COSMOS-NOSQL-1	2.83	46.6535
> 4/9/2023, 1:16:27.962 PM	COSMOS-NOSQL-1	2.83	1.9827
> 4/9/2023, 1:16:38.272 PM	COSMOS-NOSQL-1	2.83	48.8274
> 4/9/2023, 1:16:48.472 PM	COSMOS-NOSQL-1	2.83	2.2451
> 4/9/2023, 1:16:58.796 PM	COSMOS-NOSQL-1	2.83	44.8847
> 4/9/2023, 1:24:09.029 PM	COSMOS-NOSQL-1	2.83	1.8599
> 4/9/2023, 1:24:19.332 PM	COSMOS-NOSQL-1	2.83	49.2759
> 4/9/2023, 1:24:29.522 PM	COSMOS-NOSQL-1	2.83	2.2493
> 4/9/2023, 1:24:39.779 PM	COSMOS-NOSQL-1	2.83	2.0381
> 4/9/2023, 1:24:50.035 PM	COSMOS-NOSQL-1	2.83	49.3056
> 4/9/2023, 1:26:00.568 PM	COSMOS-NOSQL-1	2.83	2.6705

Figure 15-4. *KQL Query Output*

You can see from this example alone how valuable these logs become concerning the health and optimization of your workload. For instance, the same query could be rewritten to determine the most expensive queries or the longest running queries. These are hints for developers where their time optimizing will have the greatest impact. Listing 15-2 is a more advanced query which not only finds the most expensive queries but also provides the query text for them.

Listing 15-2. Top RU Consumption by Query with Query Text

```
let topRequestsByRUcharge = CDBDataPlaneRequests
| where TimeGenerated > ago(24h)
| project  RequestCharge , TimeGenerated, ActivityId;
CDBQueryRuntimeStatistics
| where CollectionName == "container1"
| project QueryText, ActivityId, DatabaseName , CollectionName
| join kind=inner topRequestsByRUcharge on ActivityId
| project DatabaseName , CollectionName , QueryText , RequestCharge,
  TimeGenerated
| order by RequestCharge desc
| take 10
```

This query is more complex, includes a join, and stores data in a variable. Let's walk through it quickly to help clarify what is going on. The *let* keyword is an assignment operator assigning the results of the first query to be used later. As you can see in our *join* statement, the "toRequestsByRUcharge" is used instead of another table like we may expect in a system like SQL. The "CDBDataPlaneRequests" table is the same table we referenced in Listing 15-1 and it provides the operation types, request charge, duration, and so on. But we often need to dig deeper. Knowing you have *a query* that costs 1,000 RUs is not as valuable as knowing *which query*.

The "CDBQueryRuntimeStatistics" table provides additional information to help our discovery such as the "PartitionKeyRangeId", that is, logical partition, "QueryText", account name, database name, and so on. But the query text is incredibly valuable as it contains the query that was submitted to the database engine.

Figure 15-5. *Query Text in Query Runtime Statistics*

If you want to determine the data storage of your logical partitions, that is, partition key ranges, you can leverage the "CDBPartitionKeyStatistics" table. This will help you identify data skew and hot partitions.

Listing 15-3. Identify Partition Key Range Storage

```
CDBPartitionKeyStatistics
| order by SizeKb desc
| where CollectionName == '<name>'
```

Finally, you can set up alerts for any query you write in your Log Analytics workspace. For instance, the max size of a logical partition is 20 GB. A query to check for partitions larger than 20 GB would look like in Listing 15-4.

Listing 15-4. Query for Partitions Larger Than 15 GB

```
CDBPartitionKeyStatistics
| where SizeKb > 15000000
```

Our goal would be to create an alert if any logical partition hits 15 GB signaling an approach to the max storage size for a logical partition. In your LAW workbook, there is a button "New alert rule", which allows you to input a query and define alert logic. For instance, if there is more than one row returned from the query earlier, send an email or SMS/push notification to someone to mitigate. Additionally, you can kick off an Azure Automation runbook, an Azure Function, Logic App, Webhook, and so on, making the alerting very flexible.

Summary

Monitoring allows us to have a better understanding of how our Azure Cosmos DB account is performing. Configuring a container, choosing a partition key, and writing documents are the first steps in your journey to understanding the service, but monitoring and logging is the first step to running your Azure Cosmos DB account in production. The Azure Portal provides Insights for your Azure Cosmos DB account and diagnostic settings allow you to export your logs to the log store of choice. I recommend configuring the diagnostic settings in your own environment and spending time to understand the data available to you. It will not be time wasted.

## CHAPTER 16

Implement Backup and Restore

Backups are a critical component to any database service. Data corruption, accidental deletion, and software bugs can all contribute to a degraded state of your data. Having a proper backup strategy in place will ensure you are able to recover your data in a timely manner. Choosing the backup policy should be based on your requirements, *RPO* (recovery point objective), and *RTO* (recovery time objective).

Azure Cosmos DB provides two backup modes: *continuous backup* and *periodic backup* to help meet the needs of your use case. It is important to understand the differences between these two modes and the limitations of restoring your data within Azure. Unlike traditional database systems, there is very little to manage for backups in Azure Cosmos DB. But understanding the functionality that is offered will ensure your data is accessible when needed. In this chapter we will discuss the different modes available and their differences.

Backup Modes

There are two backup modes in Azure Cosmos DB: continuous and periodic. Understanding which is right for your use case will determine your ability to recover data when needed. Your choice will also determine the cost of maintaining backups for your account. Backups should not necessarily be relied upon for disaster recovery (an outage of a data center or region). Azure Cosmos DB provides functionality to address high availability and disaster recovery by leveraging multiple regions, automatic failover, and data consistency levels. But, if your RPO/RTO is less strict, backup and restore can be used for DR as well as recovering from data corruption.

© Steve Flowers 2023
S. Flowers, *Designing and Implementing Cloud-native Applications Using Microsoft Azure Cosmos DB*,
Certification Study Companion Series, https://doi.org/10.1007/978-1-4842-9547-2_16

Periodic backups are the default when you first create your Azure Cosmos DB account. Backups are taken in the background and do not affect the performance of the database. Backups are stored in an Azure-managed storage account with global replication to ensure backups are available during a regional disaster. Periodic backup allows you to specify the frequency of the backups (how often you would like to take a backup) and the retention (how long to keep the backups). Both of these settings will affect your cost. Two backups are included for free, and the cost of additional copies will depend on the number of copies and the amount of data stored. The minimum backup interval is one hour.

Continuous mode backs up all changes to your account (database, container, and items) asynchronously every 100 seconds. The consistent, asynchronous backup mode provides *point-in-time* restore which allows you to select the latest restorable timestamp for a given resource. Continuous backup also occurs in the background like periodic backup and does not consume RUs or affect the performance of your account.

An important point to note: continuous mode does not support multi-region write accounts.

The retention period for continuous backup is either 7 days or 30 days. Seven days is provided at no cost but there is a cost for selecting 30 days which includes the additional storage needed to store more backups. You can choose to restore any combination of containers, shared throughput databases, or the entire account. All data restored will be consistent up to the time specified up to the restorable timestamp. Backups in continuous mode are taken in every region your Azure Cosmos DB account has configured. If you have a write region in East US, a write region in West US, and a read region in Central US, they will all be included in the backup.

Configure Backup

Configuring the backup settings for your Azure Cosmos DB account can be done in the Azure resource creation wizard or after your account has been deployed. When creating a new resource, there is a "Backup Policy" step that will allow you to select periodic or continuous. When selecting periodic, you will have to additionally configure your backup interval and retention. The minimum backup interval is 60 minutes, and the maximum is 24 hours. The minimum backup retention is 8 hours, and the maximum is 30 days. As you select your interval and retention, the portal will show you how many copies of data you will be storing. This will determine the cost of your periodic backups.

If continuous mode is selected, your options for setting the interval and retention go away. The retention period is determined by the continuous mode you select, 7 days or 30 days. The interval is 100 seconds as previously mentioned. The 7-day continuous backup is available for free, while the 30-day retention comes with additional cost. The cost is determined by the amount of data and the number of regions in your account. The following is not restored when using either backup method:

1. Firewall, VNET, data plane RBAC

2. Additional regions

3. Stored procedures, UDFs, triggers

4. RBAC assignments

If you already have an Azure Cosmos DB account that you would like to change the backup policy, this can be done in the Azure Portal. However, accounts using continuous mode cannot be converted back to periodic mode. If your account is configured for periodic mode, you can navigate to the "Backup & Restore" blade in your Azure Cosmos DB account, as depicted in Figure 16-1. This is where you can edit your interval and retention settings as well as change to continuous mode.

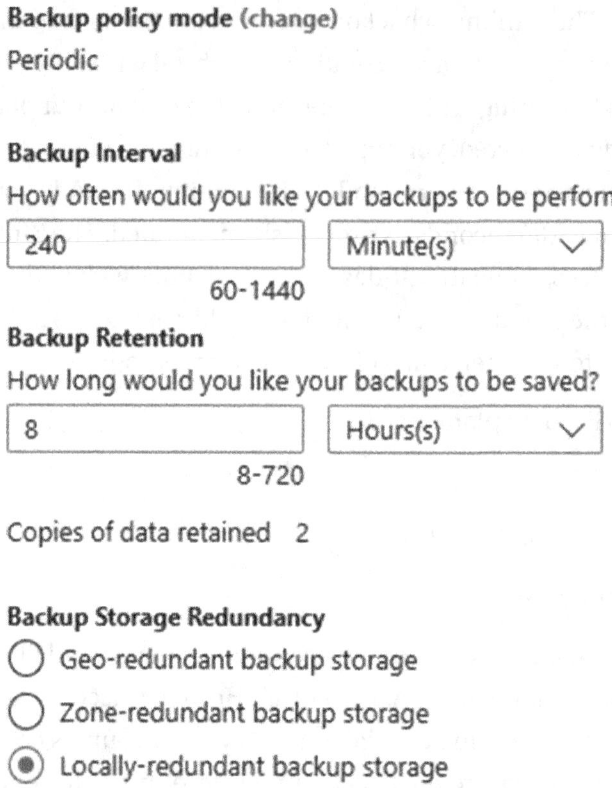

Backup policy mode (change)
Periodic

Backup Interval
How often would you like your backups to be performed?

| 240 | Minute(s)   ⌄ |

60-1440

Backup Retention
How long would you like your backups to be saved?

| 8 | Hours(s)   ⌄ |

8-720

Copies of data retained   2

Backup Storage Redundancy
○ Geo-redundant backup storage
○ Zone-redundant backup storage
◉ Locally-redundant backup storage

Figure 16-1. *Change Backup and Restore Settings*

You can also change the storage redundancy in this pane. Locally redundant means that the storage is copied within the data center three times to prevent loss of data if there is a hardware or networking failure. Zone redundant ensures that your data will be available within a region having a data center issue. And geo-redundant will ensure your data is available in the case an entire Azure region becomes unavailable.

If you select to change to continuous mode, you will be presented with the same options as the wizard, as shown in Figure 16-2.

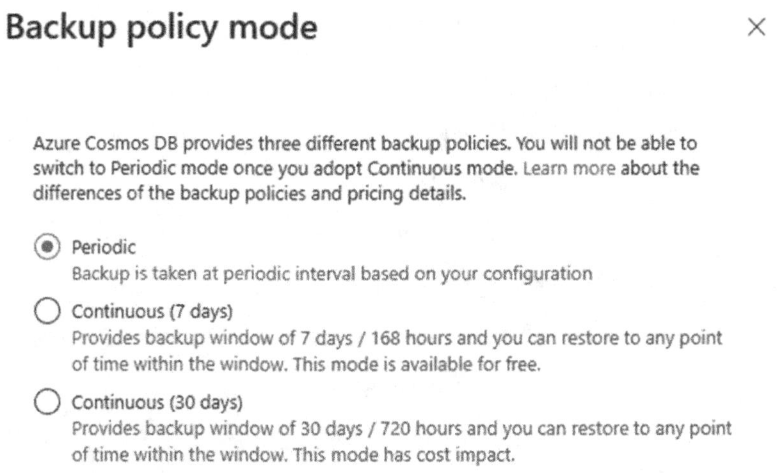

Backup policy mode ✕

Azure Cosmos DB provides three different backup policies. You will not be able to switch to Periodic mode once you adopt Continuous mode. Learn more about the differences of the backup policies and pricing details.

- ⦿ Periodic
  Backup is taken at periodic interval based on your configuration

- ○ Continuous (7 days)
  Provides backup window of 7 days / 168 hours and you can restore to any point of time within the window. This mode is available for free.

- ○ Continuous (30 days)
  Provides backup window of 30 days / 720 hours and you can restore to any point of time within the window. This mode has cost impact.

Figure 16-2. *Changing from Periodic to Continuous*

Again, once you make the change to continuous, you cannot go back to periodic.

Restore from Backup

Periodic backup requires a support ticket to restore a database or container. This is cumbersome and therefore continuous backup is recommended. When contacting support, you should be prepared to provide your Azure subscription ID, your Azure Cosmos DB account name, and the names of the databases or containers you need restored. You do not have access to the status of your restoration but will see the restored data in a new Azure Cosmos DB account.

To perform a restore for an account configured for continuous backup, use the "Point In Time Restore" (PITR) blade from the account navigation menu.

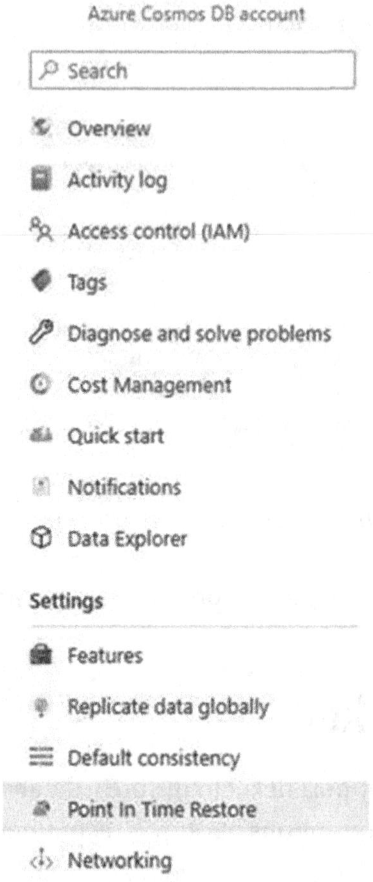

Azure Cosmos DB account

🔍 Search

💠 Overview

📋 Activity log

🔑 Access control (IAM)

🏷 Tags

🔧 Diagnose and solve problems

🕐 Cost Management

📖 Quick start

📋 Notifications

📦 Data Explorer

Settings

🔒 Features

💧 Replicate data globally

☰ Default consistency

📥 Point In Time Restore

‹⟩ Networking

Figure 16-3. Point in Time Restore

Once in the PITR menu, you will have several options to determine the data to be restored. The restore point determines the point in time that you would like to restore to. If you deployed a change that caused data corruption, select a time before the change. The restore point can either be manually entered, or you can browse the available restore points based on events that have occurred against your Azure Cosmos DB account by clicking the "Need help with identifying restore point" link. You can choose to restore the entire account or select resources.

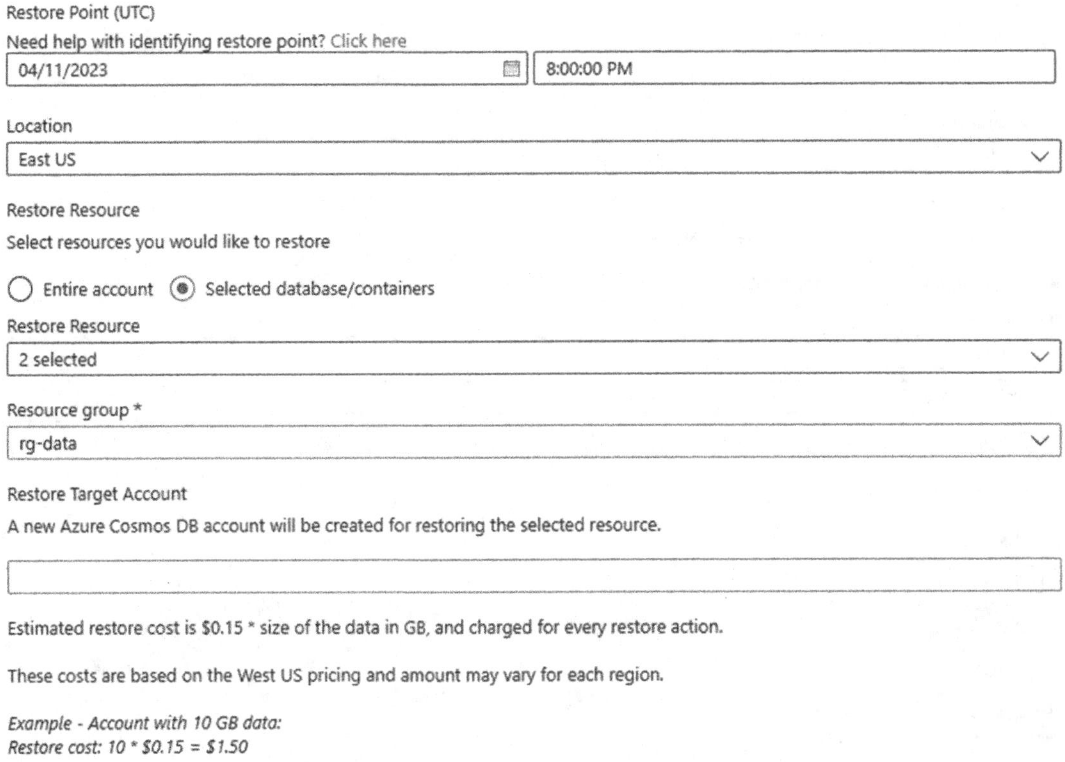

Restore Point (UTC)
Need help with identifying restore point? Click here

| 04/11/2023 | 🗓 | 8:00:00 PM |

Location

| East US | ∨ |

Restore Resource
Select resources you would like to restore

◯ Entire account   ◉ Selected database/containers

Restore Resource

| 2 selected | ∨ |

Resource group *

| rg-data | ∨ |

Restore Target Account
A new Azure Cosmos DB account will be created for restoring the selected resource.

| |

Estimated restore cost is $0.15 * size of the data in GB, and charged for every restore action.

These costs are based on the West US pricing and amount may vary for each region.

Example - Account with 10 GB data:
*Restore cost: 10 * $0.15 = $1.50*

Figure 16-4. *Point in Time Restore Options*

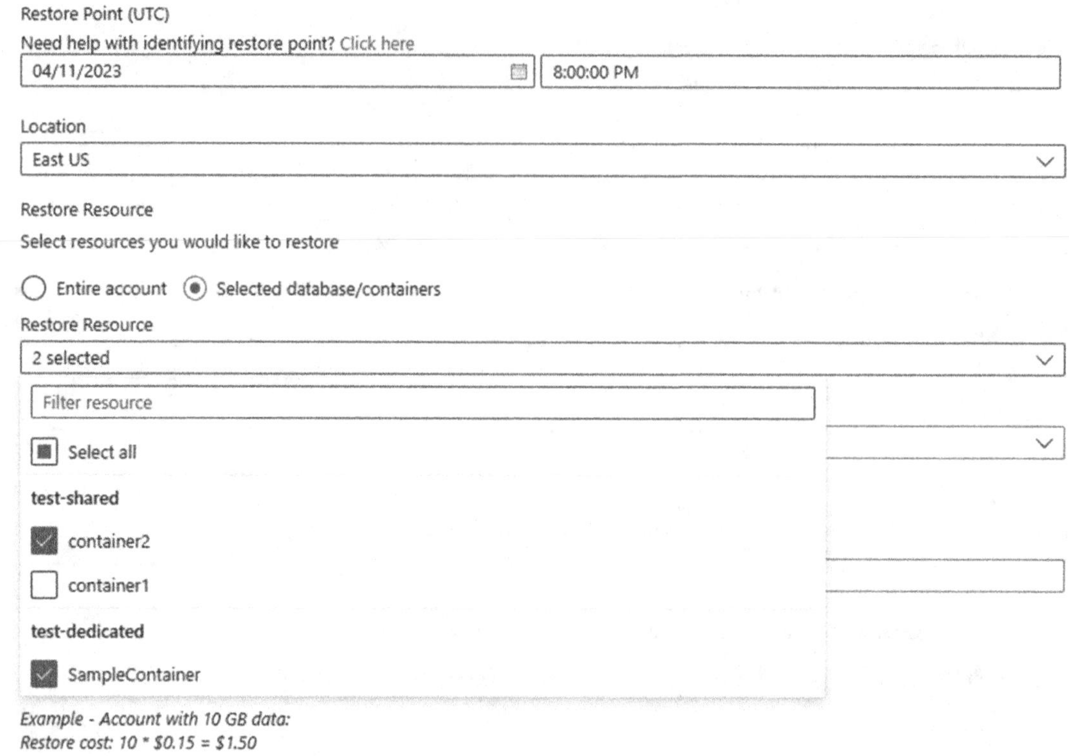

Restore Point (UTC)
Need help with identifying restore point? Click here

04/11/2023		8:00:00 PM

Location

East US	∨

Restore Resource
Select resources you would like to restore

◯ Entire account ⦿ Selected database/containers

Restore Resource

2 selected	∨

Filter resource	

■ Select all

test-shared

☑ container2

☐ container1

test-dedicated

☑ SampleContainer

Example - Account with 10 GB data:
*Restore cost: 10 * $0.15 = $1.50*

Figure 16-5. *Point in Time Restore Resource Selection*

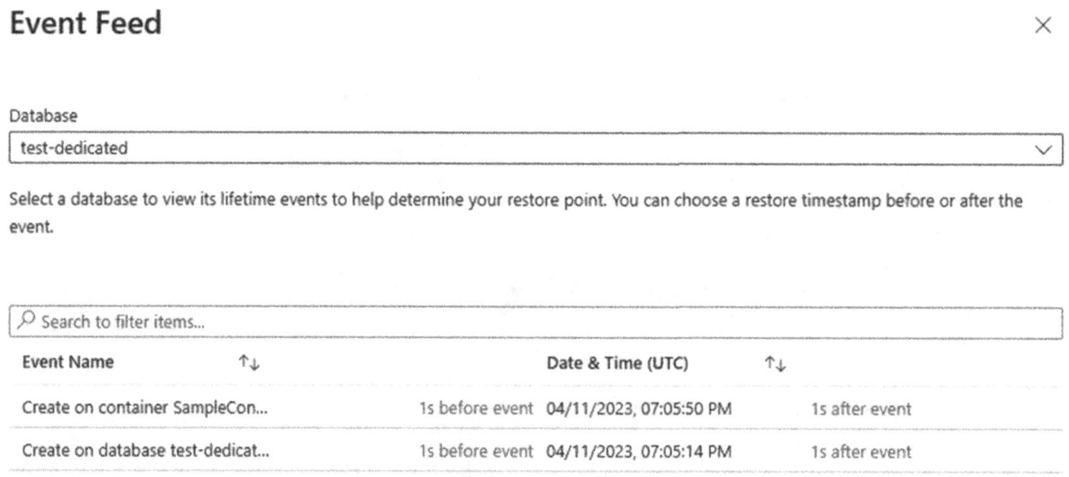

Event Feed   ✕

Database

test-dedicated	∨

Select a database to view its lifetime events to help determine your restore point. You can choose a restore timestamp before or after the event.

🔎 Search to filter items...

Event Name	↑↓		Date & Time (UTC)	↑↓	
Create on container SampleCon...		1s before event	04/11/2023, 07:05:50 PM		1s after event
Create on database test-dedicat...		1s before event	04/11/2023, 07:05:14 PM		1s after event

Figure 16-6. *Choose a Restore Point Based on the Event Feed*

Once a restore is initiated, a log entry will appear in the Activity Log of your Azure Cosmos DB account with the operation name "Restore Live Database Account" and the status of "Started". Once the restore finishes, another log will be created with a "Success" or "Failure" designation.

Operation name	Status	Time	Time stamp
⌄ ⓘ Restore Live Database Account	Succeeded	3 minutes a...	Tue Apr 11 ...
ⓘ Restore Live Database Account	Started	17 minutes ...	Tue Apr 11 ...

Figure 16-7. *Monitoring Restore Operation*

A restore operation will also restore the TTL of documents which can lead to immediate deletion of items.

Summary

Understanding your backup and restore options in Azure Cosmos DB may not be as exciting as data modeling or global high availability, but it is a critical component to successfully running your workload in production. Azure Cosmos DB offers the simpler, less flexible periodic backup model, which allows you to choose coarse grain time windows to backup and restore data. Continuous backup provides much more flexibility and point-in-time restore to ensure your data is restored to a fine-grained point in time to reduce data loss. These will be important topics to understand not only when using Azure Cosmos DB in production, but also when you are taking the DP-420 exam.

## CHAPTER 17

Implement Security

Security is paramount when considering which data store to implement for your organization's critical applications. Cloud-native services greatly benefit from the tightly coupled ecosystem in which they reside, providing less friction when implementing things like access, authorization, encryption, and network isolation. Azure Cosmos DB is no different and provides robust security controls for the modern enterprise workload.

Security of your data store spans multiple key areas: data at rest, data in motion, control plan access, data plane access, and others. How do we ensure our data is safe while stored or while being transferred to the client? How do we control who can access our data store and from where? And how can we implement these controls in a cloud-native way, removing attack vectors and gaps in human configuration which often lead to data loss?

In this chapter we will discuss how to protect your Azure Cosmos DB account using network, identity, and data access controls. We will cover configuration topics such as private networking, integrated firewalls, and data encryption. These topics are sometimes unfamiliar to the developer who is working with a data platform and are often relegated to the administrators who own the infrastructure. But a working knowledge of these concepts will not only help you secure your Azure Cosmos DB account in production but help you pass the DP-420 exam as well.

Secure Access to Azure Cosmos DB

There are two planes of control associated with your Azure Cosmos DB account: the *data plane* and the *control plane*. The control plane defines the operations that we perform to manage our Azure Cosmos DB account. Operations such as

- Default consistency model

- Backup configuration

159

© Steve Flowers 2023

S. Flowers, *Designing and Implementing Cloud-native Applications Using Microsoft Azure Cosmos DB*, Certification Study Companion Series, https://doi.org/10.1007/978-1-4842-9547-2_17

- Networking

- Database and container creation

These are the types of configurations your operations team or cloud infrastructure resources will use to manage your Azure Cosmos DB account.

Users with the appropriate role leveraging role-based access control can perform some or all the operations required to manage your account. Using roles which are integrated with Azure Active Directory is an easy way to limit the type of access your administrators have. Each service in Azure comes with a set of built-in roles that help define user access out of the box. The roles associated with Azure Cosmos DB are as follows:

- *DocumentDB Account Contributor*: Can manage Azure Cosmos DB accounts

- *Cosmos DB Account Reader*: Can read Azure Cosmos DB account data

- *CosmosBackupOperator*: Can submit a restore request in the Azure Portal for periodic backups

- *CosmosRestoreOperator*: Can submit a restore request for accounts with continuous backup mode

- *Cosmos DB Operator*: Can provision Azure Cosmos DB accounts, databases, and containers; cannot access any data

As you can see from the list, there are roles which cover the most common use cases. Cosmos DB Operator is common for administrators who can interact with the account but should not have access to the data. It is all too common that administrators can access the data of data stores, and this is bad practice. Backup and restore operators represent a smaller scope of permissions that serve disaster recovery purposes. They cannot manipulate the account or the data but can be helpful in restoring the data to a new account. And the broadest role, DocumentDB Account Contributor, can manage the account and access data. This role should rarely be used. As a side note, do not be confused whenever you see "DocumentDB" used in Azure Cosmos DB as it is a legacy name/branding for the service.

When adding a new role assignment, use the Access control (identity and access management a.k.a. IAM) pane in the portal, previewed in Figure 17-1. Here you can add individual users, Azure AD groups, service principals, and managed identities to roles on your account.

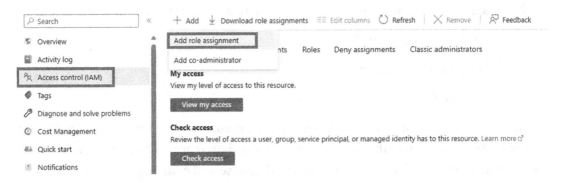

Figure 17-1. *Add Role Assignment in Azure Cosmos DB*

As discussed in previous chapters, there are keys associated with your Azure Cosmos DB account. These keys provide access to data, but they also provide access to administrative operations as well. Using the C# SDK and an account key, a developer can create a database or a container. This is not recommended for securely managed accounts and diminishes the control administrators have over the environment. To prevent this behavior, we can limit changes made from the SDKs. All accounts have a configuration property called "*disableKeyBasedMetadataWriteAccess*" which when enabled prevents account metadata access, meaning a key cannot create a database or a container. This property must be configured programmatically using ARM, Azure CLI, or PowerShell, as Listing 17-1 demonstrates.

Listing 17-1. Disable Key-Based Metadata Write Access Using Azure CLI

```
az cosmosdb update  --name [CosmosDBAccountName] --resource-group
[ResourceGroupName]  --disable-key-based-metadata-write-access true
```

Secure Access to Data

Data plane operations are defined as operations that transact data such as reading documents, writing documents, and querying documents. Unlike your operations teams, developers and their applications only need access to the data itself. In a layered security approach, there should be segregation between what the operations teams can manage and what the applications can manage. The operations team should not have access to the data but should be able to manage your Azure Cosmos DB account. The developers should be able to access the data but not change the configuration of the Azure Cosmos DB account.

There are three ways to secure access to the data in your Azure Cosmos DB account:

- Key-based access control

- Role-based access control

- Resource tokens

Key-based access control is the easiest to implement but comes with some major shortfalls. As mentioned in the previous section, key-based access provides access to operational functions of your account such as database and container creation. Most of the time this is not an ideal configuration for a secure environment. This can be limited by disabling key-based metadata access control. Additionally, key-based access is a coarse access control method. You are limited to a read/write key or a read-only key over all of the data contained in the Azure Cosmos DB account. If you implement a key-based approach, it is important to understand how key rotation works.

It is best practice to rotate your keys to prevent prolonged exposure for a single key. Your Azure Cosmos DB account comes with a primary and secondary key. When rotating your keys, you'll migrate from the primary to the secondary then regenerate a new primary (see Figure 17-2). Later, you will migrate from the secondary to the primary then regenerate the secondary key. This activity can be performed for both read/write keys and read-only keys.

Figure 17-2. *Rotating Account Keys*

Role-based access control can be used to secure the data layer as well as the control plane layer. There are only two built-in roles that can define data plane access control: Cosmos DB Built-in Data Reader and Cosmos DB Built-in Data Contributor. However, we typically want to create a customer role to define what our Azure AD user or service principal can accomplish. A custom role is required as we want to explicitly define what operations our identities can perform and at what scope. There are three available scopes: account, database, and container. These scopes define the types of operations we can perform at each level. An "item/create" rule at the account scope will allow the user to create items or documents on any database or container in the account. A security best practice is to provide least-privilege access, meaning your users should have the most limited scope of permissions possible.

The possible actions we can provide through a custom role are as follows:

- Microsoft.DocumentDB/databaseAccounts/readMetadata

- Microsoft.DocumentDB/databaseAccounts/sqlDatabases/ containers/items/create

- Microsoft.DocumentDB/databaseAccounts/sqlDatabases/ containers/items/read

- Microsoft.DocumentDB/databaseAccounts/sqlDatabases/ containers/items/replace

- Microsoft.DocumentDB/databaseAccounts/sqlDatabases/ containers/items/upsert

- Microsoft.DocumentDB/databaseAccounts/sqlDatabases/ containers/items/delete

- Microsoft.DocumentDB/databaseAccounts/sqlDatabases/ containers/executeQuery

- Microsoft.DocumentDB/databaseAccounts/sqlDatabases/ containers/readChangeFeed

- Microsoft.DocumentDB/databaseAccounts/sqlDatabases/ containers/executeStoredProcedure

- Microsoft.DocumentDB/databaseAccounts/sqlDatabases/ containers/manageConflicts

These actions can be defined for each scope allowing customization of what operations a user or service principal at each scope. Customer roles can be created using PowerShell, Azure CLI, or ARM. The first step is to create the role definition. As an example, if we want a service principal that can read, execute queries, and read the change feed in a database called "e-commerce" and a container called "orders", we may create the following role definition as provided in the Microsoft documentation.

Listing 17-2. Custom RBAC Role Definition Using PowerShell

```
$resourceGroupName = "<myResourceGroup>"
$accountName = "<myCosmosAccount>"
New-AzCosmosDBSqlRoleDefinition -AccountName $accountName `
    -ResourceGroupName $resourceGroupName `
    -Type CustomRole -RoleName MyReadOnlyRole `
    -DataAction @( `
        'Microsoft.DocumentDB/databaseAccounts/readMetadata',
        'Microsoft.DocumentDB/databaseAccounts/sqlDatabases/containers/
        items/read', `
        'Microsoft.DocumentDB/databaseAccounts/sqlDatabases/containers/
        executeQuery', `
        'Microsoft.DocumentDB/databaseAccounts/sqlDatabases/containers/
        readChangeFeed') `
    -AssignableScope "/dbs/e-commerce/colls/orders"
```

Once this new role is created, we can apply the role to a user or service principal by creating a role assignment. Again, the scope of the role assignment will define what resources (account, database, or container) the operation will succeed at. In a role assignment, the scope must match or be a subset of the scope provided in the role definition. The scope may look like as follows:

- "/" – Account level

- "/dbs/e-commerce" – Database level

- "/dbs/e-commerce/colls/orders" – Container level

You can create the role assignment using PowerShell, Azure CLI, or ARM. To create a role assignment using PowerShell, refer to the example in Listing 17-3. Notice that the scope matches the scope of our role definition (container). The role assignment in this example is constricted by the "assignable scope" property in our role definition.

Listing 17-3. Custom Role Assignment Using PowerShell

```
$resourceGroupName = "<myResourceGroup>"
$accountName = "<myCosmosAccount>"
$readOnlyRoleDefinitionId = "<roleDefinitionId>" # as fetched above
```

```
# For Service Principals make sure to use the Object ID as found in the
Enterprise applications section of the Azure Active Directory portal blade.
$principalId = "<aadPrincipalId>"
New-AzCosmosDBSqlRoleAssignment -AccountName $accountName `
    -ResourceGroupName $resourceGroupName `
    -RoleDefinitionId $readOnlyRoleDefinitionId `
    -Scope "/dbs/e-commerce/colls/orders" `
    -PrincipalId $principalId
```

RBAC will allow you to define definitions to the granularity of container level, but no lower. You cannot use RBAC to provide access at the document level, that is, read access to only a specific partition key. However, this scenario is often a requirement in enterprise applications. Consider a multi-tenant SaaS provider. They may manage many customers and the data for each customer is co-located in the same container. How do we prevent access across tenants in this scenario? The answer: Resource tokens.

Resource tokens provide specific access to partition keys, documents, attachments, stored procedures, triggers, and UDFs. In this scenario, a resource token provider is required to establish the identity and permissions of the user attempting to access data. This is commonly a mid-tier service that sits between the client and your Azure Cosmos DB instance. Once the identity of the user is established, the resource token provider requests permissions based on the identity. Resource token generation is natively handled by the SDKs, but if you are using REST, you must create the request/authentication headers yourself.

To clarify, the mid-tier service is implemented by you, the developer. There is no managed mid-tier service provided to you and you must develop your own. However, the SDK provides classes to assist in this development. The details of designing and implementing a resource token provider are out of scope for the exam and this text, but it is important to understand that resource tokens are the only way to provide document-level data plane access control to your application. Links to the Microsoft documentation on resource token providers are provided in the companion git repository and I recommend you at least give them a cursory glance.

Network Security

What layered security approach would be complete without discussing network isolation? Network security is a standard requirement for most enterprise organizations and provides a blanketed denial of access to your service based on the originating network for your requests. Azure Cosmos DB provides a built-in firewall which can be used to configure how both your public and private endpoints are exposed.

The public endpoint of your Azure Cosmos DB is a *fully qualified domain name* (FQDN) of a public endpoint that is managed by Azure. This means the public endpoint of your account is reachable from anywhere unless you restrict access using IP firewall rules. The private endpoint of your Azure Cosmos DB account is an FQDN that resolves to a private endpoint that can be connected to from your private VNETs. VNETs, or virtual networks, are networks that you have full autonomy over within your Azure environment. Think of a private endpoint as a private network interface allowing you to interact with your Azure Cosmos DB account where the packets never leave your network control.

Your IP firewall is configured in the portal from the "Networking" blade of your Azure Cosmos DB account. There is a tab for "Public access," that is, your public endpoint, and "Private access," that is, your private endpoint. There are three options for your public endpoint: "All networks," "Selected networks," and "Disabled."

The "All networks" setting requires zero configuration. Once this option is selected, any IP address with public access to the Internet can access your public endpoint. This may be beneficial for public APIs providing data to consumers, but in most cases, this should not be the configuration. The "Disabled" option totally disables your public endpoint meaning no network traffic can reach your account via the public endpoint.

The "Selected networks" option is the most common. This option provides new options for you to configure how clients can access your public endpoint. The two options provided are virtual networks (VNETs) and firewall. The virtual networks option allows you to define which internal VNETs on Azure can access your public endpoint. The firewall allows you to create a list of single IPs or CIDR ranges that can access your public endpoint. For instance, if you have a partner organization with a list of services operating on a CIDR range, you can provide them access to your public endpoint. The traffic will traverse the public Internet and reach your Azure Cosmos DB account.

There are exceptions provided for your public endpoint. The "Accept connections from within public Azure data centers" option allows you to create a blanket rule that trusts traffic originating from any Azure data center. This is certainly slightly more secure but not recommended in most cases. The "Allow access from Azure portal" option allows you to permit traffic from Azure back-end APIs. For instance, the "Insights" data for your account will be blocked if you do not check this box. That is because Microsoft manages back-end services to interact with your Azure Cosmos DB account.

Private access allows you to control access to a private endpoint. A private endpoint is an endpoint you must create which is associated with a VNET that you manage. The endpoint is then deployed to that VNET. You can then choose VNETs that can access this private endpoint. You may be asking yourself, what is the difference between this method and the public endpoint with VNET access control? The answer is ultimately name resolution. The public endpoint is an endpoint that you do not manage. Anyone can know the FQDN of your endpoint if they know your account name. They will not know the name of your private endpoint. Additionally, you must have DNS resolution in place for your private endpoints to resolve correctly making this configuration more secure, yet more tedious to configure.

Data Encryption

Data encryption ensures your data is not readable by bad actors at any point. Data at rest is defined by data in storage and data in transit is defined by data that is being transferred. Data that is in transit may be a write operation or a query that requires data be moved across a network to a client. Data at rest encryption is enabled by default for your Azure Cosmos DB account. You cannot disable this feature and AES-256 encryption is utilized. Data is also encrypted in transit via TLS (transport layer security). TLS 1.2 is the default as of April 2023 but TLS 1.0 and 1.1 are currently also supported.

For added security, data at rest can be further encrypted by a *customer-managed key* (CMK). A CMK creates an additional layer of encryption (double encryption) on top of your data beyond the service provided encryption of Azure Cosmos DB. CMKs must be stored in Azure Key vault to provide your managed key to your account. CMKs can only be configured for newly created Azure Cosmos DB accounts, so this is an important requirement to evaluate before you create your account. Once your key has been added to your Azure Key Vault instance, you are required to create an access policy that allows your Azure Cosmos DB account to read (GET) and wrap/unwrap your key. Additional reading on this topic is provided in the links for this chapter in the companion git repository.

Lastly, Azure Cosmos DB supports *Always Encrypted*. Always Encrypted allows for client-side encryption which protects secure information from ever being exposed in the database. When using Always Encrypted, the client encrypts and decrypts data client side. For instance, if a client such as an API for storing user passwords wants to securely store the password in your Azure Cosmos DB database, it may encrypt the password before ever storing it in your database. Likewise, the service will need to decrypt the data to retrieve the password. This ensures that data is never viewable in plain text to operations teams, developers, or data analysts who may have access to read data in your account.

Configure Cross-Origin Resource Sharing

Cross-origin resource sharing (CORS) is an HTTP function which allows web application requests originating from one domain to access resources in another domain. This is a popular security mechanism in web applications as it prevents malicious actors with access to a web application from using their authentication against a resource in another domain. This functionality is currently only supported for the NoSQL API in Azure Cosmos DB.

CORS can be configured in the Azure Portal by providing a comma-separated list of origin domains that are approved for CORS. Figure 17-3 displays the portal experience for configuring CORS. CORS can also be defined in your ARM template.

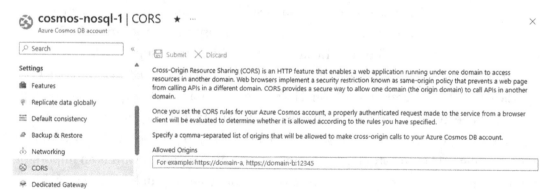

Figure 17-3. *CORS Configuration in Azure Cosmos DB*

Summary

Security is a critical component for any well-defined architecture. In this chapter, we discussed the multitude of secure configurations provided by Azure Cosmos DB. Access and authorization to your data and control plane as well as network security will be some of the first considerations you make when defining the secure configuration of your account. Azure Cosmos DB is flexible and secure providing granular controls and a layered approach to security to satisfy the requirements of your enterprise applications.

## CHAPTER 18

Implement Data Movement

Your production application leveraging Azure Cosmos DB has been live for a few months and you are beginning to see performance degradation. After analyzing the logs and performance telemetry, you determine that your data is modeled incorrectly for the current query pattern. But the primary key for a container cannot be changed after creation. You now must migrate the data to a new container, which has a partition key that supports your workload. Or another scenario, let's say that you want to migrate from the Azure Cosmos DB API for MongoDB to the API for NoSQL. How do you begin this process? Additionally, how do you integrate your Azure Cosmos DB with other services within your platform?

We've discussed how to interact with your data using the SDK and perform analytics using the analytical store and Azure Synapse Link, but there are additional scenarios you should be prepared to handle. Container migrations to change your primary key, changing APIs, and integrating with other services on your platform can all be performed using a number of technologies and methods. In this chapter we will discuss additional Azure services that can be helpful in data movement and discuss specific use cases which may be a good fit for each.

Programmatic Data Movement

In Chapter 7 we covered how to interact with your data using the Azure Cosmos DB SDK. This included the use of the Bulk Executor library. The Bulk Executor library can be very useful in data movement as it provides an easy way to take advantage of the massive throughput available to your databases and containers. The Bulk Executor library abstracts away the complexity of reaching high throughput for your application by handling rate limiting, timeouts, and exceptions natively. This can help achieve ten

© Steve Flowers 2023
S. Flowers, *Designing and Implementing Cloud-native Applications Using Microsoft Azure Cosmos DB*,
Certification Study Companion Series, https://doi.org/10.1007/978-1-4842-9547-2_18

times greater write throughput when compared to a multi-threaded application. In data movement, however, there is always a source and a destination. The Bulk Executor library helps you write to your destination, and the query iterator (as discussed in Chapter 7) helps you read from your source.

When would you want to use the SDK as your tool of choice for moving data? It likely depends on several factors. What types of resources is your team composed of: developers, data engineers, analysts? Developers would certainly prefer to use the SDK in a familiar language like C# and doing so will allow them the most control over the data movement activities.

Another factor may be the state of the system. If it is a production system that is highly critical, you may consider a *strangler fig* pattern. Strangler fig is simply defined as building an abstraction layer in front of your database while you reconfigure components on the back end. This would be difficult to accomplish without tight integration with the rest of the code base. This would allow you to perhaps move specific containers or redirect specific application processes one at a time without disrupting application functionality.

Let's consider a real-world use case. A customer I worked with used Azure Cosmos DB for the data store of their application. Initially the application was more of a "science project" where new functionality was being tested. However, it quickly became popular, and adoption increased rapidly across the organization. When evaluating the performance of the workload, it was recognized that two configurations were causing poor performance and they wouldn't be easy to correct: the partition key and the throughput provisioning model.

In this case, the customer had made an assumption about the data model that proved to be incorrect as the adoption of the application grew. As we discussed in Chapter 2, choosing the correct partitioning key will have a great impact on the performance of your application and cannot be changed after creation. However, usage patterns change, and it is important to be prepared to make changes to optimize your environment. Since the partition key cannot be changed, it was required to migrate the data to a new container with the appropriate partition key.

During our analysis, it was also discovered that the application was experiencing many 429 errors (rate limiting). The provisioning model the customer chose was to share the throughput of a database among a multitude of containers. As the adoption of the application grew, it became clear that the problem was "*noisy neighbors*," that is, the needs of a few high throughput containers were constraining the throughput of the rest. Once a container is created in a shared throughput database without dedicated throughput, it cannot be changed. This was the second reason for our migration to a new container. A new container with the proper partitioning key and dedicated throughput was created in the database.

One method to migrate to this new container, you would think, would be to use the change feed and simply set our start time to the date of the oldest document. However, for containers storing a large amount of data, this can take a long time to catch up. In our case, we needed to move data quickly. So, we opted to use the change feed for any new changes moving forward, then focus on backfilling the data that was left behind using the SDK. Using the query iterator in the SDK to read documents and the Bulk Executor to insert the documents into the new container proved to be simple and efficient for this team of developers. This method worked great, but we hit a snag. There isn't a straightforward way to control the throughput consumption for our migration activity using the SDK. Our work to copy the data to a new container was consuming too much throughput and we needed to find a method which included better control over throughput consumption: enter the Apache Spark connector for Azure Cosmos DB.

The Java SDK for Azure Cosmos DB has some added functionality for controlling throughput in your client. As such, we can leverage this functionality in Spark which is a Java-based platform. Whether you are using *Scala* or *Python*, you can control the amount of read or write throughput that is consumed for a migration job. I prefer Python personally and will demonstrate how to accomplish write throughput control in Spark.

The first step is to ensure your Spark engine of choice has the *azure-cosmos-spark* library loaded. I use Azure Synapse personally, but Azure Databricks or any other Spark engine will work just the same. The library can be loaded using the Maven coordinates:

com.azure.cosmos.spark:azure-cosmos-spark_3-2_2-12:4.18.2

These coordinates or the version of the library may be out of date depending on when you read this so make sure to use the most recent version.

Next, we need to configure our connection options. This starts by creating a configuration JSON object in Python as shown in Listing 18-1.

Listing 18-1. Write Configuration for Spark Connector in Python

```python
writeConfig = {
  "spark.cosmos.accountEndpoint" : cosmosEndpoint,
  "spark.cosmos.accountKey" : cosmosMasterKey,
```

```
    "spark.cosmos.database" : cosmosDatabaseName,
    "spark.cosmos.container" : cosmosContainerName,
    "spark.cosmos.write.bulk.enabled": "true",
    "spark.cosmos.throughputControl.enabled": "true",
    "spark.cosmos.throughputControl.name": "testing",
    "spark.cosmos.throughputControl.targetThroughputThreshold": "0.50",
    "spark.cosmos.throughputControl.globalControl.database":
    cosmosDatabaseName,
    "spark.cosmos.throughputControl.globalControl.container":
    "throughputControl",
}
```

The account endpoint, key, database, and container should be self-explanatory by now. We then enabled bulk updates, which as previously mentioned will help us chunk our data based on logical partitions and load them asynchronously improving performance.

The throughput control settings are what really define how we will limit our job from consuming too many resources on the database. As you can see, there is a setting to enable throughput control and provide a name and a database. Additionally, we need a container configured, but it is not the container we are targeting for our migration, rather tracking the work the spark engine is performing and our throughput control mechanisms. In my case, I created a new container called "throughputControl", and as jobs run, new documents are added there to track the load.

Finally, there is the "targetThroughputThreshold" which defines the maximum percentage of RUs that should be consumed during the operation. In my testing, copying five million documents against a container with 10,000 RUs took 30 minutes to complete. After setting the threshold to 50%, the time to complete the write operation was just over an hour. The write operation is performed by the "save" method on a dataframe in Spark as displayed by Listing 18-2.

Listing 18-2. Dataframe Save Operation in Spark

```
dataframe.write.format("cosmos.oltp").options(**writeConfig).
mode("append").save()
```

You can see how valuable these additional configuration operations become during a migration. You have total control over the pace of the copy and the impact to the throughput of your workload. Synapse Link using Spark and the analytical store may work for your scenario, but when latency and control are paramount, programmatic data movement using the SDK or Spark connector are the right way to go.

Low-Code Pipelines

There are plenty of scenarios where migrating our data or copying it to another data store can be performed in batch using low-code tools. Two such tools in the Azure ecosystem are Azure Data Factory and Azure Synapse Pipelines. They are mostly identical and primarily offer a low-code ETL experience for building pipelines to move data and perform light transformations. This can unlock a lot of opportunities for non-devs to interact with the data and free up critical software development resources for more impactful work.

Azure Data Factory (ADF) will consume RUs while interacting with your Azure Cosmos DB account. Unlike Synapse Link, we are connecting directly to the operational store of the account. And the first step to accomplish this in ADF is to create a *linked service*. The linked service creates the connection to your Azure Cosmos DB account. Both the API for NoSQL and API for MongoDB are supported.

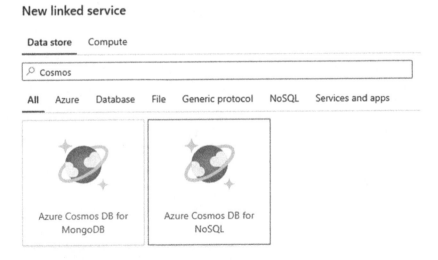

Figure 18-1. New Linked Service in Azure Data Factory

You must provide an account name and database name for the connection. The connection cannot be reused across accounts. There are several methods for authentication including the account key, service principal, or managed identities.

Once the linked service has been created, we can create a *dataset*. A dataset represents the data plane configuration of our connection, mainly defining which linked service we are using and which container to point to for reading/writing data. We don't have to define the container and can instead parameterize this field for reuse across the database.

We need to create a new pipeline in ADF, which requires you to have an ADF service deployed in your Azure subscription. In the "Author" tab of the ADF portal is where we can author new pipelines. Creating a new pipeline is as easy as right-clicking "Pipelines" and selecting "New pipeline" and a blank canvas will be created for you. In the case of data movement, let's leverage the copy data activity.

You can easily find the copy data activity by searching the "Activities" filter or finding it under the "Move & transform" group of activities. Once created, we must define our source and our sink. The sink is simply our destination for the copy activity. As you can see in Figure 18-2, I have configured a copy activity and the source settings, which includes my Azure Cosmos DB account, a dataset property for my container (parameter), and my preferred region for reading the data.

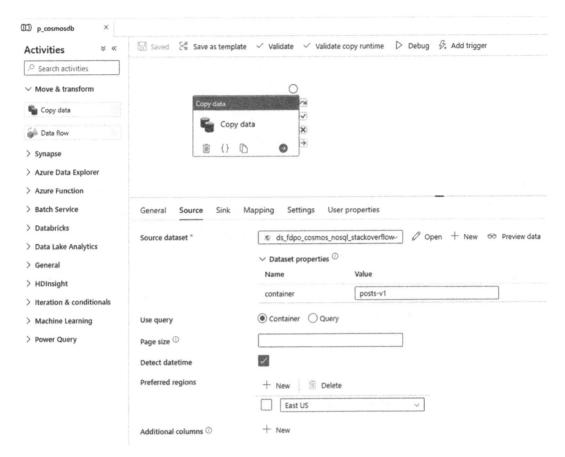

Figure 18-2. *Copy Activity Source Configuration in Azure Data Factory*

For migrating to a new container in the same account, I simply configure the same Azure Cosmos DB–linked service and dataset in the sink properties as shown in Figure 18-3.

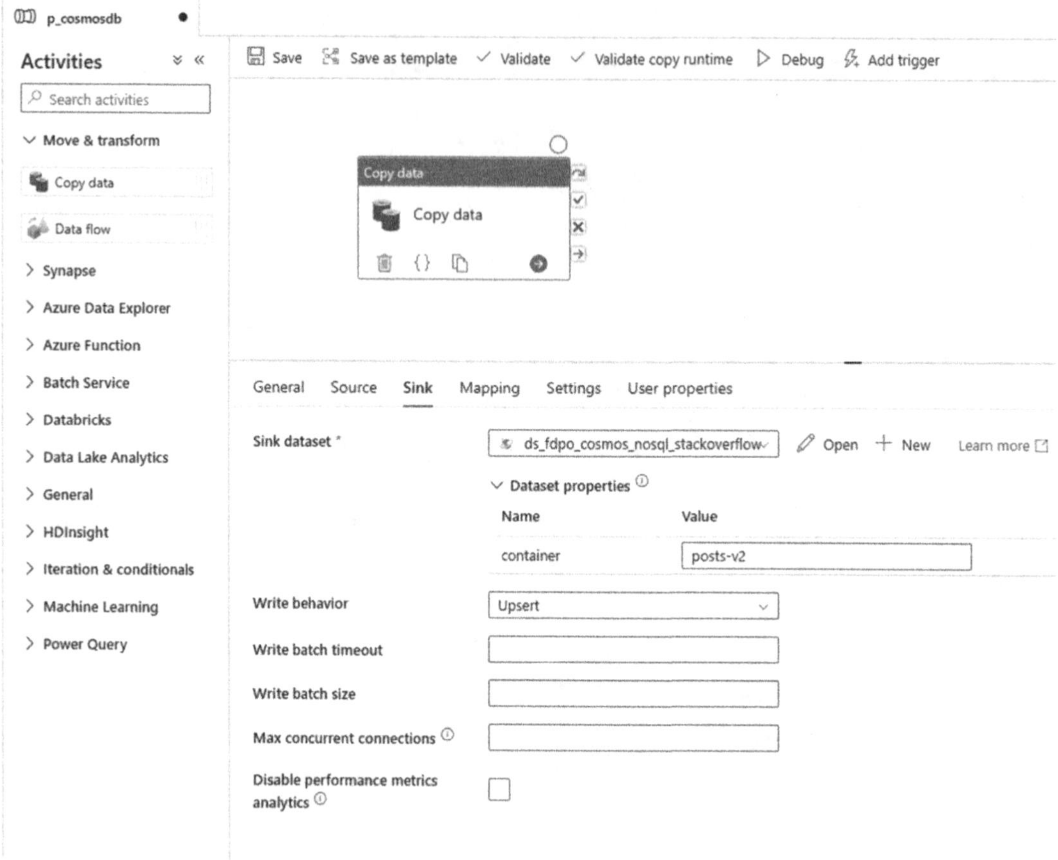

Figure 18-3. *Copy Activity Sink Configuration in Azure Data Factory*

Pretty straightforward! I've changed my dataset properties to the new "v2" container and set my write behavior to "upsert" (insert and dynamic are also supported).

The low-code approach provides very little friction to get started but offers less configuration in way of controlling your data movement activities. This may not always be the correct approach but for straightforward data movement it will certainly be faster than writing code. The lack of programming skills required to perform low-code ETL like this also means that analysts and non-developer resources can interact with the dataset without having to write a line of C#.

Streaming Data

Streaming data is everywhere these days. Whether it is IoT devices, application telemetry, or microservices, our data stores must be able to handle the volume and velocity of streaming workloads. Azure Cosmos DB is incredibly suited for streaming data workloads due to its low-latency ingestion and flexible schema. We also covered how to use the change feed to act as a stream processing feature for interacting with document changes in our databases. In this section, we'll cover two more tools to consider and have in your "streaming data toolbox" as it were.

Earlier in the book, we discussed how to integrate Azure Event Hubs with Azure Cosmos DB using Azure Functions. Another method we have for interacting with data in motion is *Azure Stream Analytics*. Where Azure Functions performed the handoff from Event Hubs to Azure Cosmos DB in our earlier examples, Azure Stream Analytics (ASA) is a low-code approach for integrating to streaming data stores. On top of that, ASA can perform micro-batch aggregations right on top of the stream using SQL.

ASA supports several source connectors: Event Hubs, IoT Hub, Blob Storage, and Data Lake Storage Gen2. As messages arrive in your Event Hub, they are ingested in batches to ASA, which then will sink them to your destination data store. While the messages are in the ASA engine, you can write queries on top of the data for real-time data analysis and transformations. You can aggregate temperature telemetry to store in Azure Cosmos DB while also triggering an Azure Function to alert support staff, or send aggregate sales data to a Power BI report while sending the full fidelity data to Azure SQL. ASA is an extremely flexible and powerful data stream processing engine.

Additionally, if your organization is heavily invested in *Kafka*, the Apache open source event streaming platform, the Kafka connector integrates with Azure Cosmos DB. This allows your organization to leverage the benefits of Kafka's scalability, customization, and message delivery features such as *exactly once* processing. Kafka Connect is a stand-alone service you must deploy and manage but connectors can be configured to integrate with Azure Cosmos DB as both a source and a sink. Providers of Kafka services like Confluent remove the hassle of managing your environment and make integration with Azure Cosmos DB even easier with its Confluent Hub CLI tools.

Summary

Data movement is a fact of life in the modern data architecture. It is critical to understand data movement in Azure Cosmos DB so your organization can be nimble and accommodate changes quickly. Whether you are correcting a mistake in your design or integrating with other platforms and services, there are many ways to interact with your data stored in Azure Cosmos DB. I recommend testing the Spark connector and understanding the various options available to you. Try to copy data from your Azure Storage account to Azure Cosmos DB, and from one container to another. Understanding data movement will provide a lot of flexibility to developers using Azure Cosmos DB on their projects as well as help you pass the DP-420 exam.

CHAPTER 19

Implementing a DevOps Process

DevOps is a set of practices that bring together developers and operations team to ensure services are deployed rapidly and reliably. This includes *CI/CD*, or continuous integration and continuous delivery. Common DevOps tools in Azure include *PowerShell, Azure CLI, Azure Resource Manager (ARM) templates*, and *Bicep templates*. In reference to Azure Cosmos DB, it is simply how you can automate the deployment and configuration of your Azure Cosmos DB and the assets therein like databases and containers.

The multimodal nature of Azure Cosmos DB means you can have a common process for deploying your accounts while having the flexibility of choosing from multiple APIs. This greatly simplifies the scripting and templating your DevOps team need to produce for your Azure Cosmos DB deployments. In this chapter, we will dive into these methods of deployment and how to apply them to your environment.

Overview of DevOps in Azure

DevOps is generally divided into *imperative* and *declarative* approaches. The imperative approach includes a well-defined method for deploying resources like an Azure Cosmos DB account where the declarative approach defines the final product and allows an intermediary to carry out the necessary tasks to reach the final state. PowerShell and Azure CLI commands would be considered an imperative approach, whereas ARM and Bicep templates would be considered declarative.

PowerShell is a general scripting language in the .NET ecosystem and Azure CLI is a command-line tool for performing administration of your Azure resources, including deployment. Both tools provide commands (or in PowerShell parlance, command-lets)

181

© Steve Flowers 2023
S. Flowers, *Designing and Implementing Cloud-native Applications Using Microsoft Azure Cosmos DB,*
Certification Study Companion Series, https://doi.org/10.1007/978-1-4842-9547-2_19

which all you to deploy your account, databases, and containers ad hoc or as part of a CI/CD pipeline.

ARM and Bicep are declarative templates that describe the outcome you wish to achieve, which can then be deployed using PowerShell, Azure CLI, or first-party and third-party tools. For example,

- Azure DevOps (first party)

- Terraform (third party)

- Ansible (third party)

Bicep is much new than ARM, and therefore, for the purposes of the exam I will focus on ARM templates in this chapter.

Common Tasks in PowerShell

PowerShell is a general scripting language in the .NET ecosystem and comes in two flavors: PowerShell and PowerShell Core. The latter operates on top of .NET core and is compatible with both Windows and Linux-based operating systems. It is installed by default on your Windows OS and can be started via the Start Menu. The Azure Cloud Shell also supports PowerShell and Azure CLI via a Bash prompt.

To get started, let's look at a PowerShell command for creating a new Azure Cosmos DB account from the Microsoft documentation as displayed in Listing 19-1.

Listing 19-1. PowerShell Create New Azure Cosmos DB Account

```
$resourceGroupName = "myResourceGroup"
$accountName = "mycosmosaccount"
$apiKind = "Sql"
$consistencyLevel = "BoundedStaleness"
$maxStalenessInterval = 300
$maxStalenessPrefix = 100000
$locations = @()
$locations += New-AzCosmosDBLocationObject -LocationName "East US"
-FailoverPriority 0 -IsZoneRedundant 0
$locations += New-AzCosmosDBLocationObject -LocationName "West US"
-FailoverPriority 1 -IsZoneRedundant 0
```

```
New-AzCosmosDBAccount `
    -ResourceGroupName $resourceGroupName `
    -LocationObject $locations `
    -Name $accountName `
    -ApiKind $apiKind `
    -EnableAutomaticFailover:$true `
    -DefaultConsistencyLevel $consistencyLevel `
    -MaxStalenessIntervalInSeconds $maxStalenessInterval `
    -MaxStalenessPrefix $maxStalenessPrefix
```

There are several variables we are initializing denoted by the $ prefix. Resource group and account name should be self-explanatory. The apiKind variable is determining which supported Azure Cosmos DB API we plan to deploy for our account. The supported values are

- Sql

- MongoDB

- Cassandra

- Gremlin

- Table

The consistency variable determines our default consistency level. The supported options are

- Strong

- Bounded staleness

- Session

- Consistent prefix

- Eventual

Just as we would expect from configuring an account manually from the portal. The maxStalenessInterval and maxStalenessPrefix are related directly to the choice of bounded staleness as our consistency model since those are configurable options when choosing bounded staleness as our default consistency level.

The next variable is an object array declared by the $locations = @() statement and where the command New-AzCosmosDBLocationObject passes its output to. The += is an assignment operator which adds objects to the object array. The fact that the command is ran twice, once with "East US" as the location and once with "West US" as the location, denotes that both regions will be deployed into during the creation of this account. To examine this, simply type it into your PowerShell terminal as shown in Listing 19-2.

Listing 19-2. Determine instance locations

```
PS /home/steve> $locations
LocationName FailoverPriority IsZoneRedundant
------------ ---------------- ---------------
East US                    0          False
West US                    1          False
```

Finally, the New-AzCosmosDBAccount command is ran which kicks off a deployment of your new Azure Cosmos DB account. You can see the status of your Azure Cosmos DB account via the Get-AzCosmosDBAccount command and update the configuration of your account with the Update-AzCosmosDBAccount command.

Creating a database and containers are the most common next steps. To perform these actions using PowerShell, we use the New-AzCosmosDBSqlDatabase command and the New-AzCosmosDBSqlContainer command. Here are examples of these commands in action. In Listing 19-3 we have created a new database with shared throughput. If we don't want shared throughput, we only need omit the -Throughput parameter.

Listing 19-3. New Database with Share Throughput Using PowerShell

```
$resourceGroupName = "myResourceGroup"
$accountName = "mycosmosaccount"
$databaseName = "myDatabase"
$databaseRUs = 400

New-AzCosmosDBSqlDatabase `
    -ResourceGroupName $resourceGroupName `
    -AccountName $accountName `
    -Name $databaseName `
    -Throughput $databaseRUs
```

To create a container, observe the command-let leveraged in Listing 19-4.

Listing 19-4. Create a New Container Using PowerShell

```
# Create an Azure Cosmos DB container with default indexes and throughput
at 400 RU
$resourceGroupName = "myResourceGroup"
$accountName = "mycosmosaccount"
$databaseName = "myDatabase"
$containerName = "myContainer"
$partitionKeyPath = "/myPartitionKey"
$throughput = 400 #minimum = 400

New-AzCosmosDBSqlContainer `
    -ResourceGroupName $resourceGroupName `
    -AccountName $accountName `
    -DatabaseName $databaseName `
    -Name $containerName `
    -PartitionKeyKind Hash `
    -PartitionKeyPath $partitionKeyPath `
    -Throughput $throughput
```

Some key parameters here are `-Throughput` and `-PartitionKeyPath`. The former configured the throughput RUs and the latter the property which is to be used as your partition key. To configure a container for autoscale throughput, the `-Autoscale MaxThroughput` parameter should be used instead, which accepts a parameter for the max throughput.

But what other tasks will be important to carry out in PowerShell? Rotating account keys is one. It is best practice to regularly rotate your account keys to ensure their security. Listing 19-5 demonstrates the command for rotating your keys provided in the Microsoft documentation.

Listing 19-5. Rotate Azure Cosmos DB Account Keys via PowerShell

```
$resourceGroupName = "myResourceGroup"
$accountName = "mycosmosaccount"
$keyKind = "primary"
```

```
New-AzCosmosDBAccountKey `
    -ResourceGroupName $resourceGroupName `
    -Name $accountName `
    -KeyKind $keyKind
```

The New-AzCosmosDBAccountKey command accepts a resource group name and an account name. Additionally, you must specify the kind of key you wish to generate such as primary, secondary, primary read only, and secondary read only.

Common Tasks in Azure CLI

In the last section we discussed the most common commands for implementing your Azure Cosmos DB account. Let's address how to perform the same work using the Azure CLI. Azure CLI is a command-line interface which implements commands that have required and optional parameters but is implemented quite differently from PowerShell. Azure CLI is also available in the Azure Portal in both the PowerShell and Bash runtime.

Creating an Azure Cosmos DB account in Azure CLI requires the use of the az cosmosdb create command. The command supports the typical parameters: resource group, account name, default consistency level, and locations. Unlike PowerShell, we must explicitly define our location information instead of building a location object. Listing 19-6 is an example from the Microsoft documentation. Two regions are deployed to just as we performed using PowerShell. In this case, we set the default consistency mode to session instead of bounded staleness.

Listing 19-6. Azure CLI Command to Create New Account

```
resourceGroupName='MyResourceGroup'
accountName='mycosmosaccount'

az cosmosdb create \
    -n $accountName \
    -g $resourceGroupName \
    --default-consistency-level Session \
    --locations regionName='West US' failoverPriority=0 isZone
    Redundant=False \
    --locations regionName='East US' failoverPriority=1 isZone
    Redundant=False
```

Notice how there does not appear to be a parameter for our chosen API? The NoSQL API is the default selection. To create an account with a different API, you must use the --kind parameter. Currently only GlobalDocumentDB (NoSQL API) and MongoDB are supported.

Azure CLI does accept objects, but not in the same manner as in PowerShell. Listing 19-7 demonstrates an operation, which updates an account to multi-write using a TSV (tab-separated values), which is returned as a string and stored to a variable.

Listing 19-7. Azure CLI Configure Account Multi-write

```
resourceGroupName='myResourceGroup'
accountName='mycosmosaccount'

# Get the account resource id for an existing account
accountId=$(az cosmosdb show -g $resourceGroupName -n $accountName --query
id -o tsv)

az cosmosdb update --ids $accountId --enable-multiple-write-locations true
```

Listing 19-8 is an example of how to create a new database for your Azure Cosmos DB account. Notice the parameters include the standard information and the throughput for shared capacity. The throughput parameter can be omitted which will not provision shared throughput at the database level.

Listing 19-8. Azure CLI Create New Database Shared Throughput

```
resourceGroupName='MyResourceGroup'
accountName='mycosmosaccount'
databaseName='database1'
throughput=400

az cosmosdb sql database create \
    -a $accountName \
    -g $resourceGroupName \
    -n $databaseName \
    --throughput $throughput
```

We can migrate, or change, the throughput for a database. In the previous example, we are using manual throughput. But we can change this account to autoscale using Azure CLI as well. Notice the command in Listing 19-9 has been extended to include the statements `sql database throughput migrate` which indicate a change in our throughput configuration.

Listing 19-9. Convert Database to Autoscale Throughput

```
resourceGroupName='MyResourceGroup'
accountName='mycosmosaccount'
databaseName='database1'

# Migrate to autoscale throughput
az cosmosdb sql database throughput migrate \
    -a $accountName \
    -g $resourceGroupName \
    -n $databaseName \
    -t 'autoscale'
```

To create a container in a NoSQL account, refer to the following command in Listing 19-10.

Listing 19-10. Create NoSQL Container Using Azure CLI

```
resourceGroupName='MyResourceGroup'
accountName='mycosmosaccount'
databaseName='database1'
containerName='container1'
partitionKey='/myPartitionKey'
throughput=400

az cosmosdb sql container create \
    -a $accountName -g $resourceGroupName \
    -d $databaseName -n $containerName \
    -p $partitionKey --throughput $throughput
```

What if you want to change regions using Azure CLI? This may be beneficial in your CI/CD pipelines if you choose to drop a region or add availability zones to a region. The command in Listing 19-11 demonstrates a manual failover and assumes the "West US" is currently your primary region.

Listing 19-11. Azure CLI to Initiate Manual Failover

```
resourceGroupName='myResourceGroup'
accountName='mycosmosaccount'

# Get the account resource id for an existing account
accountId=$(az cosmosdb show -g $resourceGroupName -n $accountName --query
id -o tsv)

# Trigger a manual failover to promote East US 2 as new write region
az cosmosdb failover-priority-change --ids $accountId \
    --failover-policies 'East US=0' 'South Central US=1' 'West US=2'
```

Listing 19-11 demonstrates that by changing the priority of "East US" to "0" you promote it to the primary, hence triggering a failover.

Deploy Using ARM Template

Finally, we have Azure Resource Manager templates, also known as ARM. An ARM template is a declarative approach where you define the desired outcome in a JSON document. The template is submitted to the Azure Resource Manager service which executes the processes necessary to facilitate the final state. You must provide parameters as you would using PowerShell or Azure CLI. Some parameters may be defined when you deploy the template at runtime, and some may be defined in the template itself.

The template will start with schema, content version, and metadata. We will ignore these configurations for now, and I suggest you reference the Microsoft docs for ARM for a deeper understanding. But we also define parameters as previously mentioned. Parameters make your templates reusable and allow you to pass in values. The accountName parameter in Listing 19-12 is an example.

Listing 19-12. ARM Template Example for Parameters

```
"parameters": {
  "accountName": {
    "type": "string",
    "defaultValue": "[format('sql-{0}', uniqueString
    (resourceGroup().id))]",
    "metadata": {
      "description": "Azure Cosmos DB account name, max length 44 characters"
    }
  },
```

Here we are defining the necessary JSON object for this parameter, which refers to the Azure Cosmos DB account name. In this case, the parameter is defining the name of the account for us with a static prefix. The actual name of the account will be sql-<Guid of your Resource Group> which makes implementing a predicable naming convention very simple. The value for resourceGroup is not provided in the template and is instead provided when the template is published.

If we look at the next parameter, we can see that the default value is provided from the command as well. If we provide the location information in a parameter, as shown in Listing 19-13, it is used in the template at deploy time and overwrites the parameter. Otherwise, the location is shared with the resource group parameter.

Listing 19-13. ARM Template Example Parameter for Location

```
"location": {
  "type": "string",
  "defaultValue": "[resourceGroup().location]",
  "metadata": {
    "description": "Location for the Azure Cosmos DB account."
  }
},
```

We can also define values, which unlike parameters are static definitions we can reference later in our configuration. They also allow you to define expressions which can be used throughout your template. Since this is a JSON document, we can also leverage the hierarchical nature of the format. In Listing 19-14 we can see how we could create our account name combining both a parameter and an expression.

Listing 19-14. ARM Template Example Variable for Account Name

```
"variables": {
  "uniqueAccountName": "[concat(parameters('Prefix'), uniqueString
  (resourceGroup().id))]"
},
```

Defining indexing policies is a great experience using ARM since they both share the common JSON format. We define an indexingPolicy object in our template with our included paths as demonstrated in Listing 19-15.

Listing 19-15. ARM Template Example Indexing Policy

```
"indexingPolicy": {
        "indexingMode": "consistent",
        "includedPaths": [
          {
            "path": "/*"
          }
        ],
        "excludedPaths": [
          {
            "path": "/myPathToNotIndex/*"
          },
          {
            "path": "/_etag/?"
          }
        ],
        "compositeIndexes": [
          [
            {
              "path": "/name",
              "order": "ascending"
            },
            {
              "path": "/age",
              "order": "descending"
```

```
            }
          ]
        ],
```

All the work we've done so far is tied together in the resources object in our template as showing in Listing 19-16. I've removed quite a lot from the following example for brevity, but you can find the full example in the Microsoft documentation or the companion git repository for this book.

Listing 19-16. ARM Template Example Resource Object

```
"resources": [
  {
    "type": "Microsoft.DocumentDB/databaseAccounts",
    ...
    "kind": "GlobalDocumentDB",
    "properties": {
      "consistencyPolicy": "[variables('consistencyPolicy')]",
      ...
  },
  {
    "type": "Microsoft.DocumentDB/databaseAccounts/sqlDatabases",
    ...
  },
  {
    "type": "Microsoft.DocumentDB/databaseAccounts/sqlDatabases/containers",
    ...
        },
        "indexingPolicy": {
          "indexingMode": "consistent",
          "includedPaths": [
            {
```

The resources object defines several object types to be included in the deployment: databaseAccounts, sqlDatabases, containers, and indexingPolicies, thus packing all of our configuration in a rather large, yet convenient JSON package.

ARM templates can be deployed in several ways. The DevOps way is a CI/CD/IaC (infrastructure as code) tool like Azure DevOps Pipelines, GitHub Actions, or Terraform. They can also be deployed using PowerShell or Azure CLI. In PowerShell, the command is `New-AzResourceGroupDeployment` and, in Azure CLI, `az deployment group create`.

Summary

There are many more commands and configurations to explore, and I highly suggest investigating the most common requirements for your deployment. To fully understand these methods, you must deploy a new Azure Cosmos DB account using PowerShell, Azure CLI, and ARM. Configure additional settings that were not covered here such as firewall rules, backup, and the analytical store. These topics will surely appear on the DP-420 exam and will greatly help your internal DevOps practices in the real world as well.

Index

A

Aggregate count, 57

Analytical workloads
  Azure Synapse Link, 103, 104
  HTAP, 101–103
  serverless SQL, 105–107
  for Synapse Spark, 107, 108

Apache Spark connector, 103, 173

ApplicationPreferredRegions, 89

Autoscale provisioned throughput, 27–29

Azure CLI, 181, 186–189

Azure cognitive search, 125, 126

Azure Cosmos DB, 1, 9, 10, 25
  account, 84, 102
  advanced SQL queries, 58–61
  buckets, 22
  change feeds, 109, 110
  database, 47
  DateTimes, 61–63
  diagnostic setting, 138, 139
  e-commerce application, 23
  emulator, 53
  failure metrics, 139, 140
  hierarchy, 22
  indexes, 127–129
  logical partitions, 23
  monitoring Insights, 140–143
  multi-region deployment, 24
  multi-region writes, 93

.NET SDK, 47–51
PaaS, 21
partition sets, 24
physical partitions, 23
properties, 60
querying logs and configuring
    alerts, 143–147
response status codes, 139, 140
SDK client options, 52–54
SQL query basics, 55–58
type check functions, 60

Azure Data Factory (ADF), 175, 178

Azure Event Hub, 138

Azure Functions, 115–118

Azure.Messaging.EventHubs, 122

Azure Portal, 42

Azure Resource Manager (ARM)
    templates, 181, 189–193

Azure service, 54

Azure Stream Analytics (ASA), 179

Azure Synapse Link, 103, 104

B

Backup
  configuring, 150–153
  modes, 149, 150
  restoring, 153–157
Bicep templates, 181
Bulk Executor, 69

© Steve Flowers 2023
S. Flowers, *Designing and Implementing Cloud-native Applications Using Microsoft Azure Cosmos DB*,
Certification Study Companion Series, https://doi.org/10.1007/978-1-4842-9547-2

Printed in the United States
by Baker & Taylor Publisher Services